INNARDS
AND OTHER
VARIETY MEATS

By Jana Allen and Margaret Gin

101 PRODUCTIONS / SAN FRANCISCO / 1974

Copyright © 1974 Jana Allen and Margaret Gin

Printed in the United States of America
All rights reserved.

Published by 101 Productions
834 Mission Street, San Francisco, California 94103
Distributed to the book trade in the United States by
Charles Scribner's Sons, New York, and in Canada
by Van Nostrand Reinhold Ltd., Toronto

Library of Congress Cataloging in Publication Data

Allen, Jana, 1942-
    Innards and other variety meats.

    1. Cookery (Variety meats)   I.   Gin, Margaret, joint
author.   II.   Title.
TX749.A683   641.6'6   73-91942
ISBN 0-912238-49-6
ISBN 0-912238-48-8 (pbk.)

CONTENTS

PREFACE

Throughout recorded history innards and other variety meats have been an important part of man's diet. They have been present on tables of both kings and peasants, worth a king's ransom at one time, relished for survival in another. Tongue, heart, brains, liver, feet, tails, etc. (called offal by the British) are some of the most flavorful of all meats and are considered to be among the greatest delicacies of culinary art.

The ancient Chinese gathered thousands of duck tongues for a single meal and the tongues of larks were a favorite of the Elizabethans. For centuries the Scots have made their haggis from the innards of deer (or sheep) mixed with onions, suet and oatmeal. Tripes à la mode de Caen and countless variations of sweetbreads are classics of French cuisine. Even our own pioneers, crossing the continent, spread their bread with the rich, buttery marrow of buffalo and served up the entrails in a hearty son-of-a-bitch stew.

However, in recent times in America, innards have often been neglected. In a land that has been spoiled by an excess of "beef and butter," they have come to be viewed as symbols of poverty. Abundance has been taken for granted and, with it, there has been an appalling waste and abuse of natural resources. We are just beginning to grasp the consequences. And, clearly, it is time for ingenuity.

That's where innards come in. They are becoming a staple in our quest for survival. Not only are they readily available, reasonably priced and highly nutritious, their uses are boundless. Once the basic cooking techniques are mastered, only the imagination limits the vast range of delicious dishes that can be created.

Quite simply, innards are begging to be understood. It is for this reason we present this book.

Jana Allen
Margaret Gin
San Francisco
June, 1974

BRAINS & SWEETBREADS

Throughout history, brains and sweetbreads have been found on the dinner table—whether esteemed as a great delicacy or eaten merely for nourishment in times of scarcity. Men of ancient times devoured the thymus (sweetbreads) of their freshly killed beasts and boiled or roasted the heads, extracting the brains, which were considered one of the best morsels of all. A dictum of the state in pre-Homerian Greece, about the fifth century, B.C., proscribed eating brains on the grounds that it was like eating the heads of one's parents. During the days of the Roman Empire, brains were used in almost every forcemeat, a preparation which survives to this day. And, though sumptuary law of the day forbade serving many variety meats at banquets, enthusiastic epicures were not curtailed for long. At the height of the Italian Renaissance, when hedonistic pleasures and extravagance reigned, such dishes as pheasant and peacock brains were highly prized and enjoyed.

According to Platina, the renowned gourmet of 15th century Italy, overindulgence in brains could bring about phlegmatic humor. He also noted that brains should always be consumed at the beginning of dinner, else risk the chance of a squeamish stomach. His book includes a recipe for the common preparation of calf brains (pickled in vinegar, mint and herbs), a dish that it was believed would increase fertility and loosen bowels if consumed by those of a warm nature. Common beliefs of the medicinal properties of brains also included the use of hare and rabbit brains as antidotes for poisons and the idea that the brains of birds were more healthful than those of beasts.

Brains and sweetbreads rose to the pinnacle of their popularity during the 19th century when the chefs of *haute cuisine* sauced them *à la Perigourdine, à la Financière, à la Nantua* or *au beurre* (or *beurre noir* for brains). Then they were found on every banquet menu of note. In the 20th century, brains and sweetbreads continue to be enjoyed. They may be scrambled for breakfast, added to forcemeats (as in the Italian *zampino*), braised in stock (Chinese brain soup) or steamed within the breast cavity of fowl. But we feel there is one serious misconception regarding brains and sweetbreads. Although they may be used interchangeably in most recipes, each has a flavor and texture distinctively different from the other. Most people who like brains will enjoy sweetbreads, but the reverse is not always true.

PREPARATION OF BRAINS

As with all soft organ meats, brains should be bought and prepared when absolutely fresh. They are very perishable and should always be eaten within 24 hours of purchasing. Fresh brains look very shiny and pinkish grey in color. The outside membrane should be moist, giving a plump, unshriveled appearance. If the brains are fresh, the outer membrane will slip easily from the meat; if they are not, the membrane has a tendency to stick to the crevices.

Step I: Soaking and Cleaning
Soak brains in cold water to cover for 30 minutes. (This step should never be eliminated.) Rinse under cold running water and drain. Remove arteries and outer membranes with a pointed knife. (Some cooks prefer to remove membranes after parboiling. Furthermore, it is not absolutely essential to remove the membrane; some cooks eliminate this step entirely.) Brains should be free of any trace of blood.

Step II: Parboiling
Parboil brains by placing them in a saucepan with cold water to cover, adding 2 tablespoons vinegar or lemon juice for each quart of water. Bring to a gentle boil, reduce heat and simmer for 5 to 15 minutes, depending on the size and variety of brains selected. Veal and lamb brains require a shorter cooking period than beef brains. Do not allow water to come to a full rolling boil. (Parboiling in acidulated water helps retain shape and whiteness.) Other ingredients may be added to the cooking liquid for flavor enrichment, if desired.

When parboiling is completed, either plunge the brains into cold water or allow them to cool in the cooking liquid. These treatments help firm up the meat, making it hold its shape when used whole or sliced for recipes. Drain well and chill brains in a covered glass jar or bowl until ready to use.

BRAIN CAVIAR

3/4 pound calf brains
white wine vinegar
3 tablespoons salad oil
1 or more cloves garlic, finely chopped
3 tablespoons lemon juice
1 teaspoon grated lemon peel
2 tablespoons finely chopped chives
2 tablespoons finely chopped
  black olives
salt and white pepper to taste
3 tablespoons chopped parsley

Soak, clean and parboil brains according to Steps I and II in basic instructions, using white wine vinegar in parboiling liquid. Immediately plunge brains into cold water; pat dry with paper towels. Press cooled brains through a sieve. Slowly combine oil with brains, stirring all the while, until mixture is smooth. Then add garlic, lemon juice and peel, chives, black olives, salt and pepper. Mound in a dish and garnish with parsley. Serve with unsalted melba toast.

BRAIN VINAIGRETTE

To make a brain vinaigrette, prepare brains as for brain caviar, omitting the olives and substituting 1 teaspoon prepared mustard, 1 teaspoon sugar and 2 teaspoons each chopped onion and chopped sweet pickle. The vinaigrette may be thinned out with a little vinegar and oil, if desired. This cold sauce is nice on salad greens as well as on cold pickled pigs' feet or tongue.

BRAIN PÂTÉ

3/4 pound calf brains
1/2 cup scalded milk
1/2 cup bread crumbs
4 eggs
1 clove garlic
3 tablespoons chopped green onions
dash of nutmeg
4 tablespoons butter
1/2 teaspoon salt
1/4 teaspoon white pepper
chopped parsley for garnish

Soak and clean brains according to Step I in basic instructions. Combine scalded milk and bread crumbs and blend well; let cool. Purée cleaned brains and eggs in a blender; add bread-crumb mixture and remaining ingredients. Pour into a well-buttered 1-quart baking dish or mold. Place in a larger pan with 1 inch of boiling water. Bake in a 300° oven for 45 minutes, or until set (when sides begin to shrink). Leave in pan 5 minutes before turning out on serving platter. Garnish with chopped parsley.

Variation: Allow baked pâté to cool slightly; then chill in refrigerator. To make aspic coating combine 1 cup clear beef stock with 2 tablespoons dry sherry or Madeira and 2 teaspoons unflavored gelatin. Cook slightly over low heat; paint entire surface of chilled pâté 4 to 5 times, chilling after each application. Garnish with chopped parsley. Serve as an hors d'oeuvre or as a first course, sliced, and placed on butter lettuce along with cornichons, Dijon-style mustard and crusty French bread.

CREAMY CHOWDER

1/2 pound veal brains
1 cup diced carrots
1 cup diced potatoes
1 cup diced celery
4 tablespoons butter
1 onion, finely chopped
3 tablespoons flour
salt and freshly ground pepper
1 cup fresh peas or corn kernels
  (optional)
2 egg yolks, beaten
2 tablespoons chopped parsley

Bring carrots, potatoes and celery to a boil with 2 quarts water; reduce heat and simmer for 30 minutes. Prepare brains according to Steps I and II in basic instructions, parboiling for 5 minutes only; dice. Then heat butter in a skillet and sauté brains with onion. Stir in flour, salt and pepper. Then add brain mixture and peas to vegetable pot, stirring all ingredients well; continue cooking 10 minutes longer. Add 1/2 cup of the vegetable stock to egg yolks, stirring constantly to prevent eggs from curdling. Just before serving, gradually add egg yolks to soup, stirring constantly. Stir in parsley and serve with crusty bread.
Serves 6 to 8

BRAIN QUENELLES

1/2 pound calf brains
1/2 cup or more bread crumbs
1/2 cup hot milk
4 tablespoons butter, softened
2 eggs
1 tablespoon sherry
1/2 teaspoon salt
dash of white pepper
dash of nutmeg

Good, hard French bread crumbs are essential to this recipe, both for flavor and texture. Thoroughly dry out bread on the kitchen counter or in the oven; then pulverize in the blender. They must be made at home; "cotton" bread cannot be substituted.
Soak, clean and parboil brains according to Steps I and II in basic instructions. Drain well and pat dry. Combine hot milk and bread crumbs together to form a smooth paste; let cool. Finely chop brains and combine with butter and bread-crumb paste until well blended. Add eggs one at a time, mixing well after each addition. Add sherry, salt, pepper and nutmeg. Adjust seasoning.
To form quenelles, roll out a scant tablespoon of the mixture, one at a time, onto a floured board and shape into sausages, about 3 inches long by 1/2 inch thick. Repeat until mixture is used up. Line quenelles in a buttered pan. Add boiling water just to cover; poach in simmering water for 10 minutes, making sure water does not boil again. Remove quenelles with slotted spoon. Place on a heated platter and serve with a curried Béchamel sauce (see Basics).
Makes 36 quenelles; serves 6 to 8 as a first course or light luncheon

Variation: Sweetbreads may be substituted for brains.

BRAINS

FRIED BRAINS

1-1/2 pounds calf or lamb brains
1 small onion
1/4 teaspoon salt
1/4 cup lemon juice
2 tablespoons olive oil
2 tablespoons finely chopped parsley
flour seasoned with salt and pepper
2 eggs, beaten
vegetable oil for deep-frying

Soak, clean and parboil brains according to Steps I and II of basic instructions, using vinegar and adding an onion and salt to parboiling liquid. Plunge into cold water. Cut cooled brains into pieces; put in a bowl with lemon juice, olive oil and parsley. Let marinate 1 hour. Drain pieces of brain and pat dry. Roll in flour, then dip into beaten egg. Deep-fry until a pale golden color in hot oil. Drain on paper towels and serve immediately with lemon wedges, tartare sauce, lemon-catsup or a catsup spiced with a dash of Tabasco and cinnamon.
Serves 6

BRAIN & SPINACH CAKES

1 pound brains (any kind)
1 cup blanched, well-drained and
    chopped fresh spinach
2 eggs
1/2 cup flour
2 tablespoons milk
1/4 teaspoon freshly grated nutmeg
salt and freshly ground pepper to taste
vegetable oil for cooking

Prepare brains according to Steps I and II in basic instructions; coarsely chop. Combine with remaining ingredients and drop by spoonfuls into hot oil, 1/2 inch deep. Brown, turning to cook evenly. Drain on paper towels. Serve with broiled or sliced tomatoes. Good for brunch or a light supper.
Serves 6

TACOS DE SESOS
(Brain Tacos)

Prepare brains according to Steps I and II in basic instructions, parboiling in a court bouillon (1 clove garlic and 2 tablespoons vinegar added to cooking liquid in addition to other ingredients). Then chop brains and sauté with onions and fresh tomatoes. Fill taco shells with this mixture, shredded lettuce, sliced radishes, sprigs of coriander and tomato salsa (see Basics).

BRAINS & HAM FOO YUNG

1/2 pound brains (any kind)
1/2 cup diced ham
4 eggs, beaten
2 cups bean sprouts
3/4 cup thinly sliced celery
2 tablespoons chopped green onions
1/2 cup chopped water chestnuts
1 tablespoon cornstarch
1 tablespoon soy sauce
1/2 teaspoon fried sesame oil*
peanut oil for cooking

Prepare brains according to Steps I and II in basic instructions; let cool and finely mince. Combine brains with ham, eggs and 2 tablespoons water; stir well. Then add remaining ingredients, blending well. Heat oil in a skillet over medium heat. When hot, add brain mixture by half cupfuls to skillet, making 3-inch pancakes. Cook 2 to 3 minutes; turn when eggs begin to set and cook until golden. Keep pancakes warm until all mixture is used. Serve with soy sauce.
Makes 12 3-inch pancakes
*The dark seasoning oil available at Oriental markets.

BRAINS & SCRAMBLED EGGS

1/2 pound brains (any kind)
1 small carrot
2 sprigs parsley
1/2 teaspoon thyme
5 peppercorns
2 tablespoons finely chopped parsley
2 tablespoons chopped chives
dash of cayenne
salt and freshly ground pepper to taste
3 tablespoons butter
6 eggs
3 tablespoons cream

Prepare brains according to Steps I and II in basic instructions, adding carrot, parsley sprigs, thyme and peppercorns to cooking liquid. Pat brains dry and cut in small dice. Combine brains with chopped parsley, chives, cayenne, salt and pepper. Sauté over medium heat in butter until slightly golden. Combine eggs and cream with wire whisk and pour into pan. Reduce heat slightly, stir from bottom of pan, in a folding manner, and cook until eggs just begin to set. Place on a heated platter. Serve with crisp bacon, if desired. Boiled parslied potatoes and asparagus tips are also good accompaniments.
Serves 4

BRAINS AU BEURRE NOIR
(Brains in Black Butter)

1-1/2 pounds brains (any kind)
1/4 pound butter
4 tablespoons fresh lemon juice
2 tablespoons chopped parsley
2 tablespoons chopped chives
1/2 teaspoon freshly ground black pepper
2 tablespoons capers, drained

Prepare brains according to Steps I and II in basic instructions, parboiling in a court bouillon. Cut in thick slices and keep warm. Make a black butter sauce by melting butter over medium heat, cooking until browned well, but not burned. Add lemon juice, parsley, chives, pepper and capers; cook 2 minutes. Adjust seasonings. Pour over warm brains.
Serves 4

BRAIN FRITTERS

1 pound calf brains
2 tablespoons butter
1 tablespoon flour
1/4 cup rich milk
salt and freshly ground pepper to taste
1/4 teaspoon freshly grated nutmeg
1 egg white, beaten
1/2 cup fine bread crumbs (or more)
vegetable oil for frying

Prepare brains according to Steps I and II in basic instructions, parboiling for 15 minutes; mince. Make a binder by melting butter in saucepan. Then add flour and blend for 3 to 5 minutes. Stir in milk and cook until smooth and thickened; cool. Combine with brains and add egg white and enough bread crumbs to form a ball. Shape into balls about the size of a walnut. Fry until golden brown in hot oil. Drain on paper towels.
Serves 4

SAUTÉED BRAINS

Sautéing brains is the most classic of all brain preparations. It is always necessary to soak and clean brains; however, parboiling is optional. (Follow Step I in basic instructions.) Brains should be drained well and dried between paper towels before proceeding with recipes.
Season the brains with salt, freshly ground pepper and paprika and then roll in flour, bread crumbs or corn-meal. Sauté them in butter, oil, bacon fat or any combination thereof, until delicately browned. Deglaze pan with a little dry white wine, if desired. Serve with lemon wedges, Worcester-shire sauce or tomato sauce.

Variations for added flavor: Rub some minced garlic into brains before dusting with flour; or flavor butter, oil or bacon fat with a small sprig of fresh rosemary or sage; or sauté fresh sliced tomatoes or mushrooms in skillet after sautéing brains and serve with brains.

BRAINS

HERB-BAKED CALF BRAINS

1-1/2 pounds calf brains
5 peppercorns
2 tablespoons vinegar
1/2 teaspoon thyme
1 teaspoon salt
1/2 onion, sliced
4 sprigs parsley
1 bay leaf
1 egg
3/4 cup flour
3 tablespoons butter
1/4 cup lemon juice
2 tablespoons chopped chives
lemon wedges

Prepare brains according to Steps I and II in basic instructions, adding peppercorns, vinegar, thyme, salt, onion, parsley and bay leaf to cooking liquid. Bring to a gentle boil, reduce heat and cook for 15 minutes. Cool in liquid and drain.
Mix egg with 2 tablespoons water. Dip brain in egg, then in flour and brown in butter. Place in baking dish, drizzle with lemon juice and sprinkle with chives. Bake at 375° until golden, about 20 minutes. Garnish with lemon wedges.
Serves 4 to 6

KOHLRABIS STUFFED WITH BRAINS

Since kohlrabis are at the peak of their season during June and July, this would make a rather special first course for a summer dinner party. However, it would also make a hearty and rich one-meal dish served on one of the first crisp fall eves.

8 young kohlrabis
1 pound calf brains
1/4 pound butter
1/2 cup chopped onions
salt and freshly ground pepper to taste
1/8 teaspoon freshly grated nutmeg
1 tablespoon chopped parsley
1 egg
1/2 pint sour cream

Carefully peel kohlrabis and hollow out center. Prepare brains according to Steps I and II in basic instructions; cut into small pieces. Heat half of the butter and sauté onions and brains 10 minutes; remove from heat. Add salt, pepper, nutmeg, parsley and egg; mix well. Stuff each kohlrabi with mixture. Place in a shallow baking dish and spoon sour cream evenly over them. Top with remaining butter. Bake in a 350° oven for 30 minutes. Serve hot. Serves 8 as a first course, 4 as an entrée

ROAST CHICKEN STUFFED WITH BRAINS

1 pound brains (any kind)
1 roasting chicken or large fryer, about 3 pounds
salt and freshly ground pepper
2 tablespoons olive oil
1/4 cup dry white wine
1 tablespoon chopped parsley
2 tablespoons chopped green onion
1 teaspoon fresh tarragon leaves, chopped
1/2 teaspoon salt
1/2 teaspoon cracked pepper
softened butter as needed

Prepare brains according to Step I in basic instructions; leave whole. Salt and pepper inside cavity of chicken. Combine remaining ingredients and marinate brains 1 hour, turning from time to time. Stuff chicken with brains, including marinade; truss with white string or skewer securely. Place chicken on a rack in a roasting pan and rub well with soft butter. Roast in a 400° oven for 1 hour, or longer, depending on size of bird. Remove brains carefully from cavity and serve along with chicken.
Serves 6 to 8

SWEETBREADS

PREPARATION OF SWEETBREADS

When selecting sweetbreads, be aware that there are 2 glands that are classified as sweetbreads. The first is the throat sweetbreads, or thymus gland, found in the neck of young mammals. These are elongated in shape and disappear as the animal matures. The other type is the heart or belly sweetbreads. These are located close to the heart and are rounded or contoured. Most cooks prefer this variety for sautéing or braising, as they are more delicate. For the same reason, veal or lamb sweetbreads are preferred to beef sweetbreads. Veal or lamb sweetbreads may be recognized by their whiteness and tenderness; beef sweetbreads have a reddish cast and are somewhat resistant to thumb pressure. Freshness is a critical factor in selecting sweetbreads, as soft gland tissue deteriorates readily from exposure. Look for moist, plump sweetbreads. Sweetbreads should be cooked within a day of purchase.

Step I: Soaking
Soak sweetbreads in cold, even icy water, to cover, for 20 minutes.

Step II: Parboiling
Place sweetbreads in cold water to cover with 1/2 teaspoon salt and the juice of 1/2 lemon added to each quart water. (Acidulated water helps retain whiteness.) Bring to a gentle boil, reduce heat and simmer for 15 minutes. Immediately plunge sweetbreads into cold water to firm up meat. Remove the tubes which connect the pair and the outer membranes; pat dry.
Note: A court bouillon also may be used for parboiling. Most often the sweetbreads are cooled in this stock for added flavor.

Ingredients for court bouillon:
1 small onion
1 stalk celery, with top
1 carrot
1/2 bay leaf
water to cover

Step III: Chilling
When sweetbreads are to be used for escalopes, after parboiling weight with a heavy plate to remove excess liquid. Place in the refrigerator for 1 to 2 hours; slice crosswise 1/4 inch thick and proceed with recipe.

SWEETBREAD SOUP WITH VERMICELLI

1 pair veal sweetbreads
1-1/2 quarts rich beef or veal stock
1 tablespoon chopped parsley
4 ounces vermicelli
salt and freshly ground pepper

Prepare sweetbreads according to Step I in basic instructions. Then simmer in stock and parsley for 20 minutes. Remove sweetbreads and chop. Return to pot with vermicelli and season to taste with salt and pepper. Cook for 5 to 7 minutes.
Serves 4 to 6
Note: Brains may be substituted for sweetbreads in the above recipe. Prepare according to Step I in basic instructions for brains.

Variation: For a Yugoslavian flavor, sieve sweetbreads. Then beat with 1 egg, 2 tablespoons lemon juice and 3 tablespoons yoghurt. Pour hot stock gradually into this mixture; return to heat for a minute or 2. Do not boil.

SWEETBREADS & CUCUMBER SALAD

1/2 pound veal sweetbreads
1/2 cup peeled and diced cucumbers
1/2 cup diced celery
1/4 cup chopped green onions
1 cup unpeeled, diced apples
1/4 cup sour cream
1/4 cup mayonnaise
1 tablespoon lemon juice
1 teaspoon sugar
chopped walnuts for garnish

Prepare sweetbreads according to Steps I and II in basic instructions; dice, making about 1 cup and chill thoroughly. Place in bowl and add chilled vegetables and apples; mix lightly. Make dressing by combining remaining ingredients. Toss lightly into sweetbread mixture. Serve on lettuce leaves, garnished with walnuts.
Serves 4

Variation: Follow the above recipe, finely mincing all ingredients. Use for a spread on open-face sandwiches.

BAKED SWEETBREADS

1 pound veal or lamb sweetbreads
4 tablespoons melted butter
1 clove garlic, finely chopped
1/2 teaspoon salt
dash of white pepper
2 tablespoons fine bread crumbs

Prepare sweetbreads according to Steps I and II in basic instructions, parboiling just 5 minutes. Split cross-wise. Dip pieces in butter mixed with garlic; season with salt and pepper. Place in shallow baking dish, drizzle with remaining garlic butter, sprinkle with bread crumbs and bake in a 350° oven for 40 minutes.
Serves 2

Variation: Equal parts of bread crumbs and freshly grated Parmesan cheese may be substituted for plain bread crumbs. Also 1/2 teaspoon chopped chives and 1/2 teaspoon tarragon may be added to bread crumbs for a spicier flavor.

DEEP-FRIED OR SAUTÉED SWEETBREADS

1 pound veal or lamb sweetbreads
1/2 teaspoon salt
1/4 teaspoon white pepper
1/8 teaspoon powdered ginger
1/2 cup fine bread crumbs
1 egg, beaten
vegetable oil for frying, or
butter for sautéing

Prepare sweetbreads according to Steps I and II in basic instructions, parboiling for 10 minutes only. Cut in 1/2-inch slices. Combine bread crumbs with seasonings. Roll sweetbreads in crumbs, dip in egg and roll once again in crumbs. Fry in hot oil, 1/2 inch deep, or sauté in butter until lightly browned.
Serves 2

BROILED SWEETBREADS

For broiled sweetbreads, follow the preceding recipe, placing sweetbreads on rack of broiling pan. Broil for about 14 minutes, turning once. Serve with lemon wedges or Hollandaise sauce, fried bacon, a grilled tomato and green salad. Broiled mushroom caps are another good garnish.

SWEETBREADS

ESCALOPES OF SWEETBREADS WITH HAM & CHEESE

1 pound veal sweetbreads
1/2 pound thinly sliced boiled ham
1 to 1-1/4 cups grated Monterey Jack
   cheese
salt and freshly ground pepper
1/4 teaspoon freshly grated nutmeg

Prepare sweetbreads according to Steps I, II and III in basic instructions; slice crosswise 1/4 inch thick. Layer sweetbreads in shallow, buttered baking dish. Top first with ham slices, then with grated cheese. Season each layer with salt, pepper and nutmeg. Place in a 450° oven and bake 15 minutes, until cheese is melted and slightly golden. Serve on hot or toasted French bread with a green salad and vinaigrette dressing.
Serves 2 to 3
Note: This is a good filling for crêpes.

SWEETBREAD CROQUETTES

1 pair veal sweetbreads, cooked and
   finely chopped (about 1 cup)
3 tablespoons butter
1-1/2 teaspoons flour
2/3 cup cream
1 egg yolk, beaten
12 mushrooms
1-1/2 teaspoons salt
1/4 teaspoon white pepper
1 teaspoon finely chopped parsley
1/2 teaspoon onion juice
beaten eggs
fine bread crumbs
vegetable oil

Prepare sweetbreads according to Steps I and II in basic instructions, parboiling them in acidulated water or court bouillon. Heat 1 tablespoon butter in a saucepan and add flour, making a roux; add cream, stirring until smooth. Add egg yolk and sweetbreads; cook 1 minute. Remove from heat.
In the meantime, heat 2 tablespoons butter in a separate skillet and sauté mushrooms quickly; remove and finely chop. Add to sweetbread mixture, along with salt, pepper, parsley and onion juice; mix well. Shape into balls about the size of a walnut, roll in beaten eggs, then into bread crumbs. Fry in deep hot oil.
Serves 4

16

BRAISED SWEETBREADS & ONIONS

1 pound veal or lamb sweetbreads
3 tablespoons butter
2 tablespoons oil
2 onions, thinly sliced
1 teaspoon flour
dash of cayenne
1-1/2 teaspoons Worcestershire sauce
1 tablespoon tomato paste
2 tablespoons dry sherry
1/2 cup chicken stock

Prepare sweetbreads according to Steps I and II in basic instructions; slice. Heat 2 tablespoons butter and 1 tablespoon oil in skillet and sauté sweetbreads until lightly browned. Remove and keep warm. Add remaining butter and oil and onions, and sauté until golden. Sprinkle with flour and stir well; add remaining ingredients. Simmer for 5 minutes. Return sweetbreads to sauce and continue cooking another 15 minutes. Serve with rice or boiled noodles or on toast.
Serves 2 to 4

Variation: Follow the above recipe, omitting tomato paste and onions. Add 1 cup finely grated carrots and 1/2 teaspoon tarragon to the pan immediately after sautéing sweetbreads.

SWEETBREADS & SCALLOPS

1 pair veal sweetbreads
4 tablespoons butter
1/2 cup sliced mushrooms
3/4 pound scallops, quartered
4 tablespoons flour
1-1/2 cups rich milk
1/4 cup dry sherry or vermouth
salt and white pepper to taste
buttered bread crumbs

Prepare sweetbreads according to Steps I and II in basic instructions; cut in pieces. Heat butter and sauté mushrooms and scallops for 5 minutes; remove with slotted spoon. Add flour to pan, making a roux; add milk, stirring constantly, until smooth and slightly thickened. Add sherry and salt and pepper. Return scallops, mushrooms and sweetbreads to sauce. Pour into individual casseroles and sprinkle with buttered bread crumbs. Bake in a 350° oven for 20 minutes. Garnish with watercress.
Serves 4

Variation: Follow the above recipe, substituting oysters for scallops.

ESCALOPES OF SWEETBREADS & ASPARAGUS

1 pound veal sweetbreads
1 egg, beaten
fine bread crumbs
2 to 4 tablespoons clarified butter
salt and freshly ground pepper
1/4 cup dry white wine
1 pound asparagus tips, steamed
    just until tender
melted butter and lemon juice

Prepare sweetbreads according to Steps I, II and III in basic instructions; slice crosswise 1/4-inch thick. Dip sweetbreads in egg, then into bread crumbs; sauté in butter until delicately browned. Season to taste. Place in circle around serving platter; keep warm. Deglaze pan with wine and pour over sweetbreads. Place asparagus in center of platter and drizzle with melted butter and lemon juice. Serve with fried potatoes.
Serves 2 to 3

Variation: Follow the above recipe, substituting buttered egg noodles or a saffron-flavored pilaf for the asparagus. Serve with a green salad.

SWEETBREADS & VEAL KIDNEYS

1 pair veal sweetbreads
3 veal kidneys, cut in small pieces
6 tablespoons butter
6 tablespoons oil
4 tablespoons finely minced shallots, or
1/2 cup minced green onions
salt and white pepper
1/2 pound button mushrooms
1/3 cup Madeira
1 teaspoon tarragon
1 teaspoon cornstarch, mixed with
2 tablespoons reserved stock
chopped parsley

Prepare sweetbreads according to Steps I and II, parboiling in court bouillon; reserve cooking liquid. Cut in small pieces. Heat 3 tablespoons each butter and oil, and sauté shallots until transparent; add sweetbreads and sauté 5 minutes longer. Salt and pepper to taste. Remove to serving dish and keep warm. Add remaining butter and oil to skillet and sauté kidneys. Add mushrooms and sauté 5 minutes. Season to taste. Remove to serving dish and keep warm. Deglaze pan with Madeira, 1 cup reserved stock and tarragon. Bring to a boil; bind juices with cornstarch mixture, stirring constantly, until smooth and thickened. Pour over meats and sprinkle with chopped parsley. Serve with rice, in patty shells (see Basics) or on buttered toast.
Serves 6

SWEETBREAD SOUFFLÉ

1 cup finely chopped cooked veal
    sweetbreads
3 tablespoons butter
3 tablespoons flour
1 cup rich milk
3 eggs, separated
1/2 teaspoon white pepper
salt
dash of nutmeg
1/4 cup grated Gruyère cheese
freshly grated Parmesan cheese

Sweetbreads should be prepared according to Steps I and II in basic instructions, parboiling in a court bouillon (for added flavor).
Preheat oven to 425°. Heat butter in saucepan; add flour, making a roux. Add milk, stirring constantly, until smooth and thickened. Stir in beaten egg yolks, sweetbreads and seasonings. Allow to cool slightly, add Gruyère.
In the meantime, beat egg whites until stiff, but not dry. Butter a 1-1/2-quart soufflé dish and dust well with Parmesan cheese. Stir 1/3 of beaten egg whites into sweetbread mixture. Then fold remaining egg whites carefully into mixture. Pour into prepared soufflé dish and put in oven. Immediately reduce heat to 375° and cook for 17 to 20 minutes for a French-type soufflé (with a soft center). For a drier soufflé, cook 30 minutes. This is beautiful served as a first course or luncheon entrée.
Serves 4

Variation: Brains may be substituted for sweetbreads. Prepare according to Steps I and II of basic instructions for brains.

SWEETBREADS SMOTHERED IN VEGETABLES

3 pairs veal or lamb sweetbreads
3 tablespoons butter
1 onion, sliced
1 carrot, sliced
1 stalk celery, sliced
1 bay leaf
1/2 teaspoon thyme
2 sprigs parsley
1 teaspoon flour
salt and freshly ground pepper
1/2 cup dry white wine
1 cup fresh peas
2 tablespoons Madeira

Prepare sweetbreads according to Steps I and II in basic instructions, parboiling in court bouillon for 5 minutes only; break in pieces; reserve cooking liquid. Heat butter in a flameproof casserole and sauté vegetables for 10 minutes until lightly browned. Stir in seasonings and flour. Salt and pepper sweetbreads and lay on top of vegetables. Add wine and 1 cup reserved stock; bring to a boil. Cover immediately and place in a preheated 350° oven for 1 hour, adjusting temperature so the ingredients are barely simmering. Baste from time to time. During last 10 minutes of cooking period, add peas and Madeira. Adjust seasonings. Serve with French bread.
Serves 6

CREAMED SWEETBREADS

1 pound veal sweetbreads
4 tablespoons butter
4 tablespoons flour
1 cup chicken stock, or
part dry white wine and stock
1 cup milk
1/2 teaspoon tarragon
dash of freshly grated nutmeg
salt and white pepper to taste

Prepare sweetbreads according to Steps I and II in basic instructions; break into pieces making about 2 cups. Heat butter in a saucepan; add flour, making a roux. Gradually add stock and milk, stirring constantly, until smooth and thickened. Add seasonings. Then add sweetbreads and heat through. Serve on fried bread rounds, toast points, in patty shells (see Basics) or over steamed white rice.
Serves 4

Variations: Pour over and/or fill omelettes and garnish with minced chives; or omit tarragon and add 1 teaspoon grated orange peel to sauce; or add 1/2 cup sliced water chestnuts just before serving; or sprinkle toasted almonds or crumbled bacon over sweetbreads just before serving; or reduce sweetbreads to 1/2 pound (about 1 cup), dice them and add 1 cup diced cooked chicken; or add 1/2 cup grated Swiss cheese to the sauce and sprinkle finished dish with freshly grated Parmesan cheese.

SWEETBREADS

SWEETBREADS & GROUND VEAL PATTIES

1 pair veal sweetbreads
1 pound ground veal
salt and freshly ground pepper to taste
2 tablespoons minced green onions
2 tablespoons finely minced parsley
1 clove garlic, minced (optional)
1 egg, beaten
2 tablespoons each butter and olive oil

Prepare sweetbreads according to Steps I and II in basic instructions, parboiling in court bouillon 10 minutes only; chop finely. Add sweetbreads to ground veal and mix with salt, pepper, green onions, parsley, garlic and egg. Form into patties and brown in hot butter and oil. Serve on split French rolls with sliced tomatoes, onions, pickles and olives.
Makes 4 to 6 patties

Variations: Follow the above recipe, substituting either ground chicken, turkey or beef for the veal.
Follow the above recipe, adding 12 to 18 mushrooms to pan after browning meat patties. Deglaze pan with 2 to 3 tablespoons Madeira and pour over all. Garnish with either parsley sprigs or watercress.
Follow the above recipe, serving crisp fried bacon with the patties. Serve with a green salad dressed with vinaigrette and crusty bread.

SWEETBREADS WRAPPED IN BACON

1-1/2 pounds lamb or veal sweetbreads
freshly ground pepper
3/4 pound bacon, blanched in
    water 5 minutes
1 onion, chopped
3 tomatoes, peeled and sliced
1 teaspoon chopped fresh sweet
    basil or parsley
1/2 cup fine bread crumbs

Prepare sweetbreads according to Steps I and II in basic instructions, parboiling in court bouillon; reserve cooking liquid. Cut in uniform pieces, about 1-1/2 x 1 inch; pepper lightly. Wrap each sweetbread piece with a strip of bacon and place in a baking dish, seam side down. Place onions, then tomatoes on top. Sprinkle with basil. Pour 1 cup reserved liquid over all and sprinkle with fine bread crumbs. Bake in a 350° oven for 40 minutes, until meat is tender. Serve with browned or boiled potatoes or boiled cabbage.
Serves 4 to 6

SWEETBREADS & OYSTER PIE

1 pound veal sweetbreads
1 pint oysters, drained and halved
2 hard-cooked eggs, sliced
3/4 cup mushrooms, sliced and
    sautéed in
3 tablespoons butter
1-1/2 cups Béchamel sauce (see Basics)
1/4 cup Madeira or dry sherry
1/4 teaspoon freshly grated nutmeg
1/8 teaspoon cayenne
2 tablespoons chopped parsley
1/2 teaspoon salt
1/2 teaspoon white pepper
biscuit pastry for 10-inch pie
    (recipe follows)
1 egg beaten with
2 tablespoons milk

Prepare sweetbreads according to Steps I and II in basic instructions, parboiling in court bouillon; slice. Layer sweetbreads, oysters, hard-cooked eggs and sautéed mushrooms in a buttered 1-1/2-quart baking dish. Combine remaining ingredients and pour over all.
Roll out pastry 1/4 inch thick on a floured board. Cut a 1-1/2-inch-wide strip and fit around rim of baking dish; cut top pastry in a round, 3/4 inch wider in diameter than baking dish. Brush rim with egg mixture and fit with top pastry. Pinch or flute edges together. Prick top well to allow steam to evaporate during baking period. Brush top with egg mixture to glaze. Bake in a 375° oven for 45 minutes, or until pastry is golden.
Serves 4 to 6

BISCUIT PASTRY

1-1/4 cups unbleached flour
2 teaspoons baking powder
1/2 teaspoon salt
3 tablespoons butter
3 tablespoons vegetable oil
1 egg, beaten

Sift flour, baking powder and salt together. Cut in butter; add oil and egg. Form into a ball, adding a little cold water if pastry is stiff. Roll out 1/4 inch thick. Use for top crust of pot pies or deep-dish pies.
Makes 1 10-inch top crust

TONGUE

Although tongue has been a popular folk food throughout the ages, it achieved its fame during the days of the Roman Empire. When snobbism and a penchant for ostentatious spending became the way of life, the Romans began to serve only the tongues of songbirds (a common meat of the day). Then, as the feasts became even more decadent, only tongues of songbirds that had been taught to say a few words were relished. At about the same time, the intrepid gourmet, Apicinus, discovered that flamingo tongues were a great delicacy.

In France in the 1300's, the first official inspection of meat transpired with the examination of pig tongues for ulcers which were thought to be the cause of leprosy. The inspectors, in fact, became known as *langueyeurs* (derived from the French *langue,* meaning tongue).

The 15th century Italian banquet always included tongue in one form or another for it was thought to be both flavorful and wholesome. We've seen recipes for salted pork tongues cooked in wine and for pickled tongue—chopped with parsley, mint, sage, spices and drowned in vinegar. Whale tongues were a common food in 16th century France. The people of the provinces braised them with lentils or peas, whereas the bourgeoisie preferred theirs spit-roasted. French gastronome de la Reynière writes of carp tongue in the 19th century. Evidently, when carp was served, the presentation began by cutting off its head. The head was always served to the most distinguished guest at the table because it contained the choicest morsel of all—the tongue! Another of his renowned colleagues, Beauvilliers, raptures over a ragout of carp tongues laced with sauce Italienne.

In America in the early 1800's, buffalo tongues were used by the Indians in bartering for whiskey from the settlers. In fact, there is one incident recorded where a band of Sioux traded 1400 buffalo tongues for a few gallons of whiskey. Actually, anywhere you find herdsmen—the Pyrénées, Australia, South America, Mexico—you will find tongue used abundantly in cooking.

PREPARATION OF BEEF (OX), CALF, LAMB AND PORK TONGUE

Step I: Cleaning

Soak tongue in cold water to cover for 1 hour. One tablespoon vinegar or lemon juice may be added for each quart water. Drain, discarding water. Some cooks prefer to eliminate this step and instead only rinse the tongues under cold, running water.

Step II: Parboiling for Calf, Lamb and Pork Tongues

Place tongue in a large pot, adding fresh water to cover, salting lightly. Parboil, uncovered, 10 minutes for small tongues and up to 30 minutes for larger ones, or until skins may be removed easily. Drain, remove skin and proceed with recipe. (Plunging a parboiled tongue in cold water makes the skin easier to remove.)

Step III: Court Bouillon for Beef (Ox) Tongues

Place tongue in large pot, adding the following court bouillon to cover. Simmer, covered, for 2 to 3 hours, or until tender. Drain and cool slightly, or allow to cool in stock for added flavor. Remove skin, gristle and excess fat from the base of the tongue. Proceed with recipes, or wrap well and refrigerate or freeze. The reserved stock may be strained and used as a soup base.

Ingredients for court bouillon:
1 onion, stuck with 2 cloves if
   desired
1 bay leaf
1 carrot
1/2 lemon (optional)
6 to 8 peppercorns
2 stalks celery, with tops
3 to 4 sprigs parsley
water to cover

TONGUE

CORNED OR PICKLED TONGUE

2 beef tongues, or
5 pounds veal, lamb or pork tongues
pickling brine (see Basics)

Wash and soak tongues in cold water to cover for 10 minutes. Place in earthenware crock or glass jar and pour in cooled brine to cover tongues. Weight with a heavy plate or clean piece of wood to keep tongues completely submerged in brine. Cover crock with loose-fitting lid or with cheesecloth. Set in a cool place 2 to 5 days, depending on variety of tongue selected and degree of corning desired. (The longer the tongues are kept in the brine, the saltier they become.)
Prepare tongue in court bouillon according to Step III in basic instructions, adding additional herbs if desired. Bring to a boil, reduce heat, cover and simmer for 1 hour for veal, lamb or pork tongues, 2 to 3 hours for beef tongues. Always check to see if meat is tender before removing from heat. Skin and serve.
Note: Tongue may be soaked overnight in cold water to remove excessive saltiness before cooking in court bouillon.

IDEAS FOR COOKED TONGUE

• Substitute tongue for ham in a Reuben sandwich. Spread mustard on slices of rye bread, then layer with tongue, sauerkraut and Swiss cheese. Butter outer sides of bread and grill on a griddle until cheese has melted and both sides are toasted.
• Layer slices of tongue, avocado and Bermuda onion on French or whole-grain bread. Spread slices of bread with mayonnaise and add alfalfa sprouts if desired.

• Layer tongue and creamed cheese or sour cream flavored with dill on whole-grain bread. Garnish with capers.
• Make croque-monsieur, using tongue. Butter outer sides of bread, then fill with a slice of Swiss cheese, a slice of tongue, strips of pimiento and another slice of Swiss cheese. Grill on a griddle until cheese has melted and both sides are golden brown.
• Cut tongue into julienne and toss in green salad of watercress or spinach and crispy bacon bits. Dress with a vinaigrette.
• Combine chopped tongue with grated onion, chopped celery and cooked rice. Bind with a little mayonnaise, flavored with lemon juice, salt and pepper. Good stuffed into tomatoes for a first course.
• Tongue is good combined with turkey, chicken, ham and/or corned beef. Use in a chef's salad dressed with a vinaigrette or Roquefort dressing.
• Combine diced tongue with cooked cauliflowerets, sliced avocado and chopped sweet red peppers. Serve with an olive oil and lemon juice vinaigrette and pile into lettuce cups.
• Chopped tongue makes a good filling for burritos.

SAUCES FOR TONGUE

There are numerous sauces, both hot and cold, that may be served with tongue. In most cases, both smoked tongue or plain boiled tongue may be used—the choice is your preference.

COLD CUCUMBER SAUCE

1 cup mayonnaise
1 cup heavy cream, whipped
1 to 2 tablespoons lemon juice
1/4 teaspoon salt
2 cups, peeled, seeded, finely
    diced cucumbers
2 teaspoons fresh chopped dill

Fold mayonnaise and whipped cream together. Stir in lemon juice and salt; then fold in cucumbers and dill. Chill well. Serve on cold sliced tongue, smoked, pickled or plain.
Makes 4 cups

WATERCRESS MAYONNAISE

1 cup mayonnaise, or
1/2 cup each mayonnaise and
    sour cream
2 tablespoons lemon juice
1 cup coarsely cut watercress
1 teaspoon sugar

Place all ingredients in blender and purée until smooth. Serve on cold sliced tongue.
Makes about 1-1/2 cups

ITALIAN SWEET & SOUR SAUCE

This sauce is similar to the Mexican molé. A surprisingly delicious taste.

1 carrot, cut up
1 onion, cut up
1 ounce bitter chocolate, in pieces
1 cup stock (reserved tongue
    stock preferred)
3 tablespoons butter
3/4 cup wine vinegar
1 tablespoon cornstarch
1/2 cup raisins
1/2 cup pitted prunes, chopped
1/2 cup pine nuts
2 tablespoons diced candied fruit
1 tablespoon sugar

Purée carrot, onion, chocolate and stock in a blender. Heat in saucepan with butter; cook, over moderate heat, 10 minutes. Combine wine vinegar with cornstarch and add to saucepan. Then add remaining ingredients and simmer another 10 minutes. Add slices of tongue and warm through.
Serves 6 to 8

TONGUE

CHILI SAUCE

1 onion, chopped
1 clove garlic
2 cups peeled, chopped tomatoes
1/2 teaspoon cumin
salt and freshly ground pepper
1 or 2 dried red chilis, or
1 or 2 teaspoons mild chili powder
2 tablespoons olive oil

Purée onion, garlic and tomatoes in blender. Add cumin, salt, pepper and chilis. Heat oil in skillet and add tomato mixture; simmer 10 minutes. Place slices of tongue on flameproof platter, pour sauce over all and simmer a few minutes to heat through. Hot tortillas and a salad of lettuce, fresh coriander, olives and radishes would be great accompaniments for this dish.
Serves 6

PORT & CRANBERRY SAUCE

1/2 cup cranberry sauce
1/2 cup Port
1 cup orange juice
1/2 lemon, cut in thin slices
4 to 6 gingersnaps, dissolved in
    orange juice
1/8 teaspoon ground cloves

Combine all ingredients in a saucepan and simmer for 10 minutes. Pour over slices of tongue and heat in a 350° oven for a few minutes. Serve with brown or wild rice.
Serves 6 to 8

ONION SAUCE

2 onions, thinly sliced
1 teaspoon sugar
3 tablespoons butter
3 tablespoons flour
2 cups beef stock
1/4 cup dry vermouth
salt and freshly ground pepper to taste

Gently sauté onions with sugar in butter for 15 minutes, carmelizing slightly. Add flour, stirring in well, and cook for 5 minutes. Then add stock, vermouth and seasonings; simmer for 10 minutes.
Place slices of tongue in baking dish, pour sauce over all and bake, uncovered, 25 minutes in a 350° oven. Serve with freshly boiled egg noodles, a green salad or cucumber and tomatoes.
Serves 6

HORSERADISH SAUCE

1 cup stock (reserved tongue
    stock preferred)
2 tablespoons freshly grated
    horseradish
2 tablespoons butter
1 tablespoon fine bread crumbs
1/3 cup cream
2 egg yolks, beaten
1 teaspoon Dijon-style mustard
salt and freshly ground pepper to taste

Simmer stock and horseradish in a
saucepan for 15 minutes. Remove
from heat and stir in butter, bread
crumbs and cream. Return to low
heat, stirring until it begins to thicken.
Slowly add egg yolks, stirring all the
while. Add mustard, salt and pepper.
Pour over warm tongue slices. Serve
with parslied potatoes and dill pickles.
Serves 6

SPANISH ALMOND SAUCE

2 tablespoons olive oil
1 clove garlic, finely chopped
1 cup peeled, chopped tomatoes
2 tablespoons chopped green olives
1/4 cup chopped blanched almonds
1/2 cup stock (reserved tongue
    stock preferred)
2 tablespoons bread crumbs
capers for garnish

Heat oil in sauté pan and cook garlic
until softened. Add tomatoes, olives
and almonds; cook 5 minutes. Add
stock and thicken with bread crumbs.
Add slices of cooked tongue and heat
through. Garnish with capers.
Serves 6

WALNUT & PEANUT SAUCE

2 or more fresh green chilis, seeded
1/2 cup walnuts
1/2 cup peanuts
1/8 teaspoon ground cloves
1/4 teaspoon cinnamon
1 onion, chopped
1 clove garlic
1/4 cup bread crumbs
3 tablespoons peanut oil
2 cups stock (reserved tongue
    stock preferred)
salt and freshly ground pepper to taste

Purée chilis, walnuts, peanuts, spices,
onion, garlic and bread crumbs in
blender. Heat oil in skillet and add
purée; cook 5 minutes. Add stock, salt
and pepper and cook until slightly
thickened. Add slices of tongue and
heat through.
Serves 6

TONGUE

TONGUE EN GELÉE

1 whole beef tongue, cooked and
    skinned
1 tablespoon unflavored gelatin
2 cups consommé
2 tablespoons dry sherry
julienne-cut strips of pimiento,
    cooked carrots and string beans,
slices of hard-cooked egg and olives
    as needed

Drain and weight tongue (with a heavy
plate) overnight in the refrigerator to
remove excess moisture. Chill vegetables. Dissolve gelatin in 2 tablespoons cold water. Add to consommé
and melt over low heat; add sherry and
cool until partially set. Paint a layer of
consommé over tongue; chill. Paint
decorations with some of the partially
set consommé. Place decorations on
tongue as desired. Repeat painting of
entire tongue several times. Pour remaining consommé in shallow pan;
chill and dice. To serve tongue, garnish
with watercress and surround with
diced consommé.

TONGUE IN ASPIC

2 tablespoons unflavored gelatin
1/4 cup dry white wine
1 cup tomato juice
2 cups clear stock (tongue stock
    preferred)
1/2 cup seeded, chopped cucumber
3 tablespoons chopped bell pepper
1 cup minced, cooked tongue
    (any kind)
2 tablespoons lemon juice
1 teaspoon chopped fresh basil, or
1/2 teaspoon dried basil
freshly ground pepper to taste

Soften gelatin in wine. Heat, stirring,
until dissolved. Add tomato juice and
stock; refrigerate until partially set.
Combine remaining ingredients with
partially set gelatin. Pour into a
1-1/2-quart mold. Chill until set. Unmold and serve on a bed of watercress
and accompany with a lemon mayonnaise or sour cream.
Serves 6 to 8

TONGUE MOUSSE

2 cups ground cooked tongue
   (any kind)
2 tablespoons unflavored gelatin
1/2 cup cold water
1-1/2 cups beef bouillon
6 tablespoons mayonnaise
1 teaspoon Dijon-style mustard
2 teaspoons Worcestershire sauce
4 tablespoons grated onion
2 tablespoons minced parsley
2 tablespoons lemon juice
2 teaspoons fresh chopped dill
dash of cayenne
1/2 cup heavy cream, whipped

Soften gelatin in cold water. Bring bouillon to a boil; add to gelatin and stir until dissolved. Chill until partially set. Combine meat with mayonnaise, mustard, Worcestershire, onion, parsley, lemon juice, dill and cayenne. Add to gelatin mixture. Then fold whipped cream into meat mixture. Pour into lightly oiled 4-cup mold. Chill until set. Unmold on bed of butter or red lettuce leaves. Serve with horseradish sauce (following).
Serves 6 to 8

HORSERADISH-SOUR CREAM SAUCE

1/2 pint sour cream
1/4 cup mayonnaise
2 tablespoons prepared horseradish
pinch of sugar

Combine all ingredients and mix well.

TONGUE-STUFFED EGGS

1/2 cup chopped boiled or smoked
   tongue (any kind)
8 hard-cooked jumbo-size eggs
1/4 cup chopped celeriac
1/4 cup finely chopped cornichons
1 cup mayonnaise
1 teaspoon dry mustard
salt and freshly ground pepper to taste

Parboil chopped celeriac for 2 minutes. Drain and cool. Cut eggs in half lengthwise; remove yolks. Combine yolks with remaining ingredients in a mixing bowl; mix well. Stuff into egg-white halves.
Makes 16 appetizers

TONGUE PASTIES

1-1/2 cups finely minced cooked
   tongue (any kind)
1/2 cup cream
1 egg white, beaten
1/2 teaspoon white pepper
pastry for 2-crust pie (see Basics)
1 egg yolk, diluted with
1 tablespoon water

Combine the tongue, cream, egg white and pepper. Roll out pastry dough 1/8 inch thick and cut in 2-1/2-inch circles. Place about 1 tablespoon filling on each circle and fold over to form half moon; press edges together with tines of a fork. Brush with egg-yolk mixture. Place on an ungreased cookie sheet in a 375° oven for 15 minutes, or until golden.
Makes 18 to 24 pasties
Note: Phyllo dough may also be used with this filling. Cut phyllo into 2x12-inch strips and brush with melted butter. Place a small spoonful of filling onto lower corner of strip. Begin folding into triangles, in flag-folding style, brushing with melted butter as you are folding; brush completed triangle with butter. Place on greased cookie sheet in a 400° oven for 15 to 20 minutes, or until puffed and golden brown.

PICKLED LAMB TONGUES

8 to 10 lamb tongues
2 to 3 sprigs parsley
2 teaspoons tarragon
1 bay leaf
1 tablespoon salt
14 peppercorns
1 onion, sliced
2 cloves garlic
4 whole allspice
1/2 cup white wine vinegar
1/2 cup water
salt to taste

Clean tongues and put into large stock pot with parsley, 1 teaspoon of the tarragon, bay leaf, salt, 8 of the peppercorns, onion, garlic and water to cover. Bring to a boil; reduce heat, cover and simmer about 1 hour, or until just tender. Drain and skin tongues (they will feel hot to the touch). Cut in half lengthwise. Place in crock or jar.

Combine remaining tarragon and peppercorns, allspice, vinegar, water and salt to taste in a small saucepan; boil 1 minute. Pour over peeled lamb tongues in crock. Let cool. Then store in refrigerator overnight to allow flavors to blend. Excellent served as a first course or on a country buffet table with mustard or horseradish.

HASH BROWN POTATOES & TONGUE

An old favorite with a new twist, but keep the accompaniments traditional —eggs sunny-side up or poached, maybe a broiled tomato. All would be hearty fare for a Sunday brunch or supper.

2 strips bacon, chopped
2 cups diced, cooked tongue
   (any kind)
4 cups cooked, grated potatoes,
   about 2 pounds
1 onion, finely chopped
salt and freshly ground pepper to taste

Heat skillet and brown bacon until crisp. Remove bacon pieces to drain on paper towel; bacon fat remains in skillet. Combine cooked bacon, tongue, potatoes and onion; add to skillet and press flat over bottom of skillet. Cook over medium heat until golden brown on underside. Carefully turn over and brown top side. Slide onto warm platter; sprinkle with salt and pepper. Serve with eggs.
Serves 4

LAMB TONGUES VINAIGRETTE

8 lamb tongues
vinaigrette (see Basics)
1 hard-cooked, finely sieved egg
   for garnish

Prepare lamb tongues according to Steps I and III in basic instructions, simmering them in the court bouillon for only 1 hour; remove skin and split lengthwise. Place in bowl and pour vinaigrette over all. Marinate in refrigerator for 12 to 24 hours, turning from time to time. Arrange tongues on platter and garnish with egg before serving.

TONGUE IN THE POT

1 beef tongue, about 3 pounds
1 pound marrow bones, cut in
    1-1/2-inch pieces
1 clove garlic
1/2 teaspoon rosemary
6 turnips, scraped and cut in chunks
6 carrots, scraped and cut in chunks
12 pearl onions
6 to 8 new potatoes
6 whole leeks, white parts only
salt and freshly ground pepper to taste

Prepare tongue according to Steps I and III in basic instructions, adding marrow bones, garlic and rosemary to court bouillon and omitting lemon. Remove any scum that forms on top. Add vegetables during the last 45 minutes of cooking period. Remove tongue and skin; cut in 1/2-inch slices. Remove vegetables and marrow bones with a slotted spoon. Place tongue slices on a warm serving platter, surrounded by the vegetables and the marrow bones, if desired. Serve with small dishes of horseradish, mustard and cornichons. Strain the broth and serve in cups separately.
Serves 6

TONGUE & SPINACH ROLLS

12 thin slices cooked beef tongue
1-1/2 cups chopped, cooked spinach
1 tablespoon butter, melted
salt and freshly ground pepper to taste
pinch of nutmeg
1 tablespoon prepared horseradish
1 teaspoon Dijon-style mustard
3/4 cup heavy cream

Combine spinach, butter, salt, pepper and nutmeg. Place a spoonful of the mixture on each tongue slice and roll up, securing with toothpicks. Place rolls in a buttered casserole. Combine horseradish, mustard and cream and pour over all. Bake in a preheated 400° oven for 20 minutes.
Serves 4

BEEF TONGUE EN PAPILLOTE

1 beef tongue
3 tablespoons butter
2 tablespoons finely chopped parsley
2 tablespoons finely chopped chives
1/2 teaspoon tarragon, bruised
4 large mushrooms, finely chopped
1 cup chopped, cooked chicken meat
2 tablespoons dry sherry
2 tablespoons tomato paste
6 slices prosciutto
watercress sprigs for garnish

Prepare tongue according to Steps I and III in basic instructions. Then slice tongue diagonally in 6 1/2-inch-thick slices, trying to obtain the largest possible slice. (Use leftover tongue in recipes calling for ground, cooked tongue.) Heat butter and sauté parsley, chives, tarragon, mushrooms and chicken meat for 5 minutes, browning slightly. Add sherry and tomato paste and blend well. Cool mixture slightly. Spread herb-chicken mixture on each slice of tongue. Cover with prosciutto and place each of the prepared tongue slices on a piece of buttered parchment (brown paper may be substituted), fold and seal edges by turning under. Put on a buttered shallow baking dish and bake in a 350° oven for 30 minutes. For serving, place papillotes on a heated serving platter and cut away upper layer of paper with a sharp knife. Garnish with watercress and serve with broiled tomato halves.
Serves 6

Variation: Follow the above recipe, substituting 1/2 cup well-drained chopped spinach and 1/2 cup cooked, ground veal for the chicken meat.

FEIJOADA

This dish probably more than any other, has made Brazilian cooking internationally known. Although we've used tongue, salt pork and chorizo, any number of meats may be added from pigs' tails to pork cutlets.

1 beef tongue, about 3 pounds
2 cups Latin American black beans
1/2 pound salt pork, blanched
    2 minutes and diced
1 bay leaf
1 teaspoon crushed oregano
1/2 pound chorizo sausage, sliced
4 tablespoons lard
2 cloves garlic, finely chopped
1 onion, chopped
1 or more dried red chilis, minced
1 tablespoon grated orange rind
orange slices

Prepare tongue according to Step I in basic instructions. Wash and soak beans overnight. Drain, discarding water. Return beans to pot with water to cover, salt pork, bay leaf, oregano and tongue; simmer, covered, 1-1/2 hours. Then add chorizo and continue cooking 30 minutes longer. When tongue is tender, remove from pot, skin and slice thinly. Drain beans, reserving liquid.

Heat lard and sauté garlic, onion and chili until onions are transparent. Add drained beans; mash and fry, adding more lard and reserved liquid if necessary to keep beans from drying out. Fry over low heat for 30 minutes or more. Place beans in center of heated platter and surround with tongue slices and chorizo. Garnish with grated orange rind and orange slices. Serve with tortillas and a bowl of tomato salsa (see Basics).
Serves 8

CHILI-TONGUE RELLENOS

8 strips cooked tongue (any kind)
8 fresh long green chilis
1/2 pound Monterey Jack cheese,
    cut into 8 strips
flour
vegetable oil for frying
batter (following)

Tongue may be cooked by simmering in a court bouillon according to Step III in basic instructions, or by simmering in lard (see burritos, page 81). Skin chilis by placing on a cookie sheet and putting in a 450° oven for several minutes, until chilis are well blistered but not burned. Immediately place in a brown paper bag, close tightly and allow chilis to steam in their own moisture for 10 minutes. Remove from bag, make a lengthwise slit in the chilis and remove seeds.

Wrap chili around a slice of tongue and a piece of cheese. Roll in flour. Heat oil, 1/4 inch deep, in a skillet. Place 2 tablespoons of the batter into the pan, forming a chili shape. Place wrapped chili on top of batter and spoon an additional 2 tablespoons over top of chili. Fry until golden on underside; turn and brown other side. Repeat until all chilis and batter are used, being careful not to crowd chilis in pan. Drain on paper towels and serve with hot tomato salsa (see Basics).
Serves 4

Batter

4 egg yolks, beaten until thick
1/4 cup unbleached or all-purpose
    flour
4 egg whites, beaten stiff
pinch of salt

Gradually add flour to beaten egg yolks. Then fold in egg whites and salt. This is a good fritter batter as well.
Makes enough for 8 chilis rellenos

SMOKED TONGUE
WITH TOMATILLOS

1 smoked beef tongue
3 tablespoons lard
1 onion, chopped
2 cloves garlic, finely chopped
16 small new potatoes, unpeeled
4 to 5 long green chilis, peeled,
    seeded and chopped
1-1/2 pound tomatillos, cut in
    small wedges
2 tablespoons chopped fresh coriander
salt and freshly ground pepper

Prepare tongue according to Steps I
and III in basic instructions, simmering
in court bouillon. Cool in cooking
liquid; remove tongue, skin and slice;
reserve liquid. Line an ovenproof casserole with sliced tongue. Heat lard
and sauté onion and garlic until transparent. Add potatoes, chilis, tomatillos
and coriander and cook and stir for 5
minutes over medium heat. Add mixture to casserole along with enough
reserved stock just to cover the tongue
and potatoes. Season with salt and
pepper. Cover casserole and place in a
350° oven for 20 to 25 minutes, or
until tomatillos have practically disin-
tegrated.
Serves 6 to 8

BROILED TONGUE
WITH ANCHOVY BUTTER

1 beef tongue, about 2 to 3 pounds
1 teaspoon anchovy paste
4 tablespoons butter, softened
2 tablespoons French bread crumbs
2 slices raw bacon, chopped

Prepare tongue according to Steps I
and III in basic instructions; slice 1/2
inch thick. Combine anchovy paste
and butter; spread on each slice of
tongue and place in a buttered shallow
baking dish. Sprinkle bread crumbs
and bacon over all; place under broiler
until bacon is crisp and bread crumbs
are slightly browned, about 10 minutes. Serve with baked potatoes.
Serves 4 to 6

CALF TONGUES
WITH VEGETABLES

4 calf tongues
2 tablespoons each vegetable oil
    and butter
2 onions, sliced
4 carrots, sliced
1/4 pound mushrooms, sliced
1 cup beef stock
1/2 cup sour cream
2 tablespoons flour
1 teaspoon salt
1/4 teaspoon cracked pepper
1/4 teaspoon nutmeg
1 tablespoon chopped parsley
1/4 cup chopped sweet gherkins

Prepare tongue according to Steps I
and II in basic instructions, parboiling
just 15 minutes. Skin and cut into
1/4-inch slices. Heat oil and butter in
flameproof casserole and sauté tongue
until lightly browned. Add vegetables
and stock; cover casserole and place in
a 325° oven for 1 hour, or until
tongues are tender. Heat remaining
ingredients in a saucepan and bring
almost to a boil. Slowly stir into
tongue mixture; return to oven and
continue cooking for another 15 minutes. Serve with freshly boiled
potatoes or Swedish rye bread.
Serves 4

TONGUE

STUFFED TONGUE

1 beef tongue, about 3 to 4 pounds
1/2 cup lemon juice
1/2 pound ground veal
1/2 pound ground pork sausage
1/2 cup minced ham
2 hard-cooked eggs, chopped
2 eggs, beaten
1-1/2 teaspoons salt
1/2 teaspoon freshly ground pepper
2 tablespoons chopped fresh
    coriander or parsley
1 teaspoon crushed oregano
1 bay leaf
1 onion, quartered
6 peppercorns
1 cup white wine

Clean tongue and dry with paper towels. Make a deep lengthwise slit on the underside of the tongue almost to the tip. Then make several lengthwise slashes in the flesh of the meat. (This gives a nice design in cross section slices.) Then rub lemon juice into meat and let stand 10 minutes.

In the meantime, make a forcemeat by combining the veal, pork sausage, ham, hard-cooked eggs, beaten eggs, 1/2 teaspoon salt, pepper and coriander. Pile forcemeat onto flesh of tongue. Now enclose mixture in tongue by pulling cut sides of tongue together and sewing with trussing needle that has been threaded with heavy thread. Don't be afraid to pull skin slightly as it is quite elastic. The forcemeat must be securely fastened.

Place stuffed tongue in large pot; add oregano, bay leaf, onion, peppercorns, 1 teaspoon salt, wine and water to cover, about 1-1/2 quarts. Cover and simmer 2 hours. Remove tongue, reserving liquid. Let tongue stand for 10 minutes before skinning and slicing. Serve with hot tomato salsa (see Basics). This dish is also delicious served cold.

Serves 6 to 8

Note: Make a delicious soup for the next day by straining the reserved stock and adding 2 cups peeled diced tomatoes and 1/2 cup cooked rice. Simmer 30 to 40 minutes or until rice is cooked.

BRAISED TONGUE
WITH OYSTER SAUCE

1 beef tongue, about 2 pounds
1 slice fresh ginger root
4 whole star anise
1 teaspoon fennel seeds
1 tablespoon salt
2 tablespoons peanut oil
1 to 2 cloves garlic, finely chopped
1/4 cup oyster sauce*
1/4 cup dry sherry
1 tablespoon sugar
1/4 teaspoon 5-spice powder
1 cup reserved stock
1 cup sliced bamboo shoots or
    water chestnuts
1 tablespoon cornstarch, mixed with
1/4 cup cold reserved stock
fresh coriander and chopped green
    onions for garnish

Prepare tongue according to Step I in basic instructions. Cover with fresh cold water and add ginger root, star anise, fennel seeds and salt. Bring to a boil, cover and simmer about 1 hour, or until meat is tender. Remove from pot, discard skin, cut in half lengthwise and then into 1/4-inch slices. Reserve stock.

Heat oil in a large skillet or wok. When it sizzles, add garlic and brown lightly. Then add, while stir-frying, tongue slices, oyster sauce, sherry, sugar, 5-spice powder and reserved stock. Cover and simmer over low heat 15 minutes. Add bamboo shoots and continue cooking another 5 minutes. Thicken juices with cornstarch mixture, stirring slowly into pan. Garnish with coriander and onions and serve with steamed rice.
Serves 6 to 8
*Available in Oriental markets

POZOLE

Originally made from the pig's head, this popular Mexican and Southwestern pork stew can vary according to the cook's taste. It is often served after a night of merriment.

1 pork or veal tongue
1 pound pork loin, cut in pieces
1 stewing chicken, disjointed
3 pig's feet, split
2 onions, chopped
4 to 6 cloves garlic
2 or more tablespoons New Mexico
    chili powder
1 pound nixtamal hominy*,
    well rinsed
salt

Prepare tongue according to Step I in basic instructions. Clean pig's feet according to Step I in basic instructions, page 93. Cook tongue, pork loin, chicken, pig's feet, onions and garlic with 3 quarts water for 1 hour, covered. Add chili powder and nixtamal and continue cooking until all meats are tender, about 1 to 1-1/2 hours longer. Remove tongue, skin and cut in pieces. Return to pot and salt to taste. Serve in soup plates with hot tortillas and bowls of lime wedges, sliced radishes, chopped red onions, shredded lettuce and salsa. Each person adds condiments according to his own taste.
Serves 6 to 8
*White fermented corn available in Mexican markets.

HEART

The heart may be singled out as the most neglected variety meat of all, mostly because of the prejudices that have long been associated with it. Up until about the first century, B.C., heart, and for that matter, all offal, were savored by hunters and warriors. It was a custom of the tribe to reserve the heart, liver and kidneys for the chief or young warriors as these organs were thought to build strength and courage.

Then superstitions slowly began to filter into men's thoughts. So much so, that by classical Greek and Roman times, some innards were actually proscribed. By the 15th century, heart, in particular, was still in disfavor among diners. The Italians of that day considered the heart the reserve of melancholy and feared that eating it would interfere with their dedication to cultural pursuits, religious pilgrimages and enjoyment of life.

In another part of the world, in the Aztec civilization of Mexico, the living human heart was thought to be the finest offering a man could make to the gods. The Aztecs believed the gods drew strength from the human heart, a thought not far removed from that of his primitive brother. The hearts of animals, however, were not involved in religious sacrifices.

Heart is a versatile meat, tasting a bit like tongue, but with a crisp, tender texture. Contrary to popular opinion, it is not odd tasting, nor is it strong in smell or flavor. It is found throughout the cuisines of many cultures, but mostly in slaughter day specials or prairie dishes such as son-of-a-bitch stew; in pasties or meat pies such as those often served in the British Isles; or at feasts where the entire carcass of an animal is spit roasted such as in the days of the Caliphate or at Italian and Greek Easter celebrations. The South Americans are known for their *anticuchos* (marinated pieces of heart that are threaded on skewers and grilled), and the Northern Europeans have served up heart in any number of braised dishes for hundreds of years.

PREPARATION OF HEART

Heart requires very little preparation. Wash it thoroughly in cold, running water, but do not soak it. Then remove any hard connective tissue and arteries with a sharp knife. Heart is as tender as kidneys and liver, and may be sautéed quickly and served pink in the center. However, if cooked beyond this point, the meat toughens. Few cooks realize this fact. Consequently, heart more often is cooked slowly, for an extended time by moist heat methods—braising, stewing or in casseroles or ragouts. For extra tenderness, heart should be sliced lengthwise first, then cut across the grain for cooking.

PICKLED HEART

Prepare heart—any kind in any amount —according to basic instructions in preparation; cut in 1-inch cubes. Parboil for 15 minutes in water to cover with 1 stick cinnamon and a little salt. Let cool in cooking liquid; drain well. Pour vinaigrette (see Basics) over heart. Place in jars with tight-fitting lids. Refrigerate. May be stored up to 1 week in the refrigerator. Eat as hors d'oeuvre or with salads. Add to cold meat plate.

BROILED CALF HEART

After washing heart and removing arteries, pat dry and cut calf heart in half, lengthwise. Then cut in slices about 1/2 inch thick. Broil with a piece of bacon wrapped around each slice for a total of 10 minutes.

Variations: Press freshly cracked pepper into each side of heart steak. Let stand for 30 minutes or longer to absorb flavors. Wrap with bacon and broil as directed above. Or eliminate bacon and sear in a hot skillet. When you turn steak over, place a pat of butter on top. Then squeeze a little lemon juice and a drop of Worcestershire sauce over the top. Remove steak and keep warm. Deglaze pan with Cognac. Pour sauce over steak. Serve immediately.

37

HEART

STUFFED LAMB HEARTS WITH APPLES

4 lamb hearts
3 tablespoons vegetable oil
2 cups bread crumbs
4 tablespoons melted butter
1/2 cup finely chopped celery
1/2 cup chopped onions
1-1/2 teaspoons fresh sage leaves
1/4 teaspoon marjoram
salt and freshly ground pepper
4 baking apples, peeled and cored
1 cup dry red wine

Prepare hearts according to Step I in basic instructions. Heat oil and sear hearts well. Combine bread crumbs, butter, celery, onions, sage, marjoram, salt and pepper in a bowl. Stuff mixture into pocket of hearts and into cored apples. Place hearts in center of baking dish and surround with apples. Pour wine over all. Bake in a 350° oven for 1-1/2 hours.
Serves 4

BAKED HEART WRAPPED IN CAUL

4 lamb, pork or veal hearts, about
    1/2 pound each
1 teaspoon 5-spice powder
2 tablespoons each dry sherry
    and soy sauce
3 green onions, cut in 2-inch lengths
4 sprigs fresh coriander
1/4 pound caul (leaf fat)*

Remove arteries, veins and excess fat from hearts. Combine 5-spice powder with sherry and soy and rub well into cavity and outer sides of hearts. Divide green onions and coriander into 4 portions and stuff into cavity of each heart. Wrap each heart securely with a piece of caul. Place seam side down in a baking dish. Bake in a 375° oven for 1 hour. Serve with rice or barley and a watercress and orange salad.
Serves 4
Note: This may also be served as one of several dishes—Chinese family style —by slicing into bite-size pieces.
*The fatty membrane investing the intestines.

VEAL HEARTS WITH WITH SOUR CREAM

2 pounds veal hearts (about 4)
3 tablespoons butter
1 onion, chopped
1/4 pound fresh mushrooms,
    thinly sliced
1 cup chicken stock
1/4 cup Madeira
salt and freshly ground pepper
1/2 pint sour cream

Prepare hearts according to Step I in basic instructions; slice thinly. Heat 2 tablespoons butter in a flameproof casserole and sauté onion until transparent. Add remaining butter, mushrooms and hearts and sauté lightly. Add stock and Madeira; season to taste. Cover and cook in a 325° oven 1 hour, or until hearts are tender. Stir in sour cream and cook 5 minutes longer. Serve with buttered egg noodles.
Serves 4

KOFTA

1 pound lamb heart, ground
1 pound lean ground lamb
1 onion, finely minced
1 egg, beaten
1/2 teaspoon ground cinnamon or
    allspice
1/2 teaspoon ground coriander, or
1 tablespoon chopped fresh coriander
salt and freshly ground pepper

Combine all ingredients and place in refrigerator for 2 hours to allow flavors to blend. Shape into patties or sausages, and grill over charcoal or broil, to desired doneness. To serve, pile in pocket of Arab bread along with tomatoes, radishes, cucumbers and bell peppers. Spread hot sauce over all.

Serves 6 to 8

Note: Traditionally, kofta are molded in sausage-shaped balls around skewers and grilled.

SWEET & SOUR HEART

1 beef heart, about 4 pounds
1 cup white wine
1 cup wine vinegar
2 onions, sliced
2 carrots, sliced
1 bay leaf
1 teaspoon peppercorns
2 whole cloves
4 whole allspice
2 tablespoons sugar
flour
3 tablespoons each butter and oil
1 cup crushed gingersnaps
1/2 cup raisins

Remove arteries and excess fat from heart; leave whole and place in earthenware or china bowl. Combine wine, vinegar, 1 cup water, onions, carrots, bay leaf, peppercorns, cloves, allspice and sugar in a saucepan and bring almost to a boil. Pour over heart and let marinade cool, turning meat from time to time. Refrigerate at least 3 days, turning meat each day.

Remove heart from marinade and pat dry. Dust lightly with flour. Heat oil and butter in Dutch oven and brown meat on all sides. Add marinade to pot. Bring to a boil, reduce heat, cover and simmer for 2-1/2 hours. Remove heart to a heated platter and keep warm. Slice after 5 minutes. Strain and reserve stock.

In the meantime, make the sauce. Return 2 cups strained stock to pan along with gingersnaps and raisins. Cook together 5 minutes and serve with heart. Serve with potato pancakes, dumplings or parslied potatoes.

Serves 8

HEART

HEARTY BURGERS

1-1/2 pounds beef heart, ground
3 tablespoons chopped onion
3 tablespoons chopped bell pepper
1 tablespoon chopped parsley
1 teaspoon Worcestershire sauce
1 to 1-1/2 teaspoons freshly cracked
    pepper

Combine heart, onions, bell peppers, parsley and Worcestershire. Form into 4 patties. Press cracked pepper generously into patties. Broil or grill over charcoals to desired doneness. Serve on hot French rolls with sliced tomatoes and avocados.
Serves 4

HEART & ASPARAGUS STIR-FRY

1 pound heart (any kind)
1 tablespoon each soy sauce and
    dry sherry
1 slice fresh ginger root, minced
1 clove garlic, finely chopped
1/2 teaspoon sugar
1/2 teaspoon salt
3 tablespoons peanut oil
2 pounds asparagus, tough ends
    removed and sliced diagonally
    1/4 inch thick
1 tablespoon cornstarch, mixed with
1/4 cup water

Remove arteries and veins from heart; cut in 1-1/2-inch lengthwise strips. Then slice diagonally 1/8 inch thick. (If chicken hearts are used, leave whole.) Toss heart in soy, sherry, ginger, garlic, sugar and salt; marinate for 1 hour. Heat wok and add 2 tablespoons oil. Stir-fry heart over high heat until it begins to lose its redness. Remove to plate.
Add another tablespoon oil to wok and stir-fry asparagus for 30 seconds, stirring constantly. Add 1/2 cup water, cover and let steam rise to top. Return meat to wok, continuing to stir for 30 seconds. Bind juices with the cornstarch mixture. Serve with hot rice.
Serves 4

Variations: Broccoli, cauliflower, green beans or zucchini may be substituted for the asparagus; or toss 1 tablespoon black beans (dow see), mashed, with marinade, reduce soy sauce to 1 teaspoon and omit salt; or omit soy sauce from the original recipe and add 1 tablespoon hoisin sauce and a pinch of 5-spice powder; or omit soy sauce from the original recipe and add 1 tablespoon oyster sauce.

MONGOLIAN LAMB HEART ON SKEWERS

4 lamb hearts
2 tablespoons hoisin sauce*
1 tablespoon soy sauce
1 tablespoon dry sherry
1 tablespoon sugar
1 tablespoon peanut oil
1/4 teaspoon 5-spice powder
1/8 or more teaspoon cayenne
1 onion, cut in 1-inch pieces
1 bell pepper, cut in 1-inch pieces
toasted sesame seeds

Remove arteries and excess fat of heart; cut in 1-inch pieces. Combine hoisin, soy, sherry, sugar, oil, 5-spice powder and cayenne in a bowl and marinate heart for 2 hours, turning occasionally. Skewer heart alternately with pieces of onion and bell pepper on bamboo or metal skewers. Grill over hot charcoal about 7 minutes on each side, turning frequently to prevent burning. Baste with any leftover marinade. Sprinkle with sesame seeds just before serving. Serve with steamed rice, a slice of fresh pineapple or orange slices and garnish with watercress or coriander.
Serves 4 as an entrée; 6 to 8 as an appetizer
*Available in Oriental markets

HEART À L'ORANGE

4 pork or lamb hearts
2 tablespoons each butter and
 vegetable oil
2 slices bacon, cut in 1-inch pieces
1 clove garlic, finely chopped
2 onions, chopped
2 tablespoons butter
2 tablespoons flour
2 cups chicken stock
3/4 cup white wine
1/4 cup orange marmalade
1/2 cup orange juice
2 tablespoons orange rind,
 in thin julienne
3 tablespoons Grand Marnier,
 Curacao or Cointreau

Prepare hearts according to Step I in basic instructions; leave whole. Heat butter and oil in skillet and brown the hearts and bacon pieces. Add the garlic and onions and sauté until onions are transparent. Transfer to baking dish or casserole. Add 2 tablespoons more butter to skillet, stir in flour and gradually add stock, wine, marmalade, juice and rind. Stir constantly until smooth and thickened slightly, about 5 minutes. Add the liqueur and pour sauce over hearts. Bake in a 325° oven for 1 hour, basting occasionally. Serve with boiled potatoes or rice pilaf and a watercress salad.
Serves 4

HEART BOURGUINONNE

2 pounds heart (any kind)
1/4 pound salt pork, parboiled
 5 minutes and cut in 1/2-inch dice
1 cup beef stock
1 cup Burgundy wine
1 bouquet garni (see Basics)
1 carrot, grated
1/2 teaspoon freshly cracked pepper
2 tablespoons butter
1 cup pearl onions
1/2 pound mushroom caps
2 carrots, cut in chunks
1 cup fresh peas
1/4 cup chopped parsley for garnish

Remove arteries and excess fat from heart. Heat salt pork in a flameproof casserole. Stir occasionally and sauté lightly until fat is rendered (about 2 tablespoons); remove with a slotted spoon. Add the diced heart and sauté until golden on all sides. Add reserved salt pork, stock, Burgundy, bouquet garni, grated carrot and pepper. Bring just to a boil, reduce heat and simmer, uncovered, for 1-1/2 hours.

Melt butter in a skillet and sauté onions, mushrooms and carrot chunks for 5 minutes. Add to the pot; continue cooking for 20 minutes longer. During last 5 minutes of cooking period, add the peas. Remove bouquet garni and garnish casserole with parsley. Serve with buttered noodles or rice, a green salad, French bread and a good Burgundy. Fruit and cheese will complete the menu.
Serves 6 to 8

41

LIVER

Since history began, liver has ranked above all other offal as one of man's most prized culinary delights. Its heritage is illustrious—whether savored by young warriors after a kill, or mixed with truffles and Cognac for fine *pâtés de foie gras*. In the *Li-Chi,* a handbook of ritual during China's Han era (202 B.C. to 220 A.D.), liver was listed as one of the Eight Delicacies. The liver of a dog (then a commonplace food of China) was wrapped in a thin casing of its own fat, roasted, then seared at the last minute to give it a crisp finishing texture. Soothsayers of Homerian times made prophecies by consulting the shape and condition of a sacrificial animal's liver. The gourmet of Caesar's day, Apicius, discovered that the liver of a pig increased greatly in size if the animal was force-fed ripe figs and surfeited with honey and wine. And, according to Pliny, Romans coveted geese solely for their livers. Up until the time that the Romans conquered Gaul, geese were declared sacred animals because they had signaled warning when the Gauls attacked the Capitol. However, once this dictum was withdrawn, geese were also fattened on figs and surfeited with wine and honey.

From recordings of Marco Polo's adventures to the Far East we find that people in the mountains of Yunnan, bordering the valley of Szechwan, ate the livers of mutton, buffalo and poultry. The liver was chopped in a garlic-pepper sauce and eaten raw. Perhaps this was a forerunner of steak tartare.

In medieval times, cooked foods were sold at marketplaces for the first time, forcemeats of liver being among them. Forcemeat balls and timbales of forcemeat soon began appearing with regularity at banquet tables.

Parisian menus, by the 14th century, included first courses such as cod liver-filled pastries; Platina describes a 15th-century Italian dish made from heads, feet and entrails (liver and lung) of capons and hens that was mixed with aromatic herbs and spices and bathed in vinegar; and *The Compleat Housewife,* 1727, lists many hot hors d'oeuvre consisting of liver and kidneys as well as many other offal.

The French, however, truly began to understand the value of goose liver in the late 18th century. According to the epicure, Alexandre Dumas, the Alsatians blinded geese, nailed their feet to the floor and stuffed them with nuts until their livers reached a size 10 to 12 times that of normal size. These livers were then blended into one of the greatest delicacies known to man, *pâté de foie gras.* Antonin Carême, master chef and founder of *la grande cuisine* (classic French cookery), permanently seated *foie gras* in grandeur by using it with truffles in soups, filling it into canapes made of *pâté feuilletée,* layering it over meat *en croûte* and subtly and succulently blending it into mousses.

To this day, practically every cuisine has a liver specialty—the Jewish chopped chicken liver, the Greek *kokoretsi* (lamb intestines wrapped around skewered liver and other variety meats) or the Finnish *maksalaati aako* (a liver pudding traditionally served for breakfast or brunch).

LIVER

PREPARATION OF LIVER

Liver requires a minimum of preparation whether you are dealing with chicken livers or beef, pork or lamb liver. Usually the butcher has already removed the thin membrane that encases the liver before placing it on the counter. However, if this has not been done, simply loosen the membrane by using a sharp pointed knife. Liver should never be soaked in water prior to cooking.

If liver is to be braised or roasted in 1 piece, remove the membrane and wipe with a damp cloth. If liver is to be baked or grilled in 1 piece, either lard with fatback in 3 or 4 places, place strips of bacon over the top or rub with vegetable oil to prevent drying out. Liver contains little fat and therefore needs constant moisture. Basting will produce the same results.

Liver should be cooked over medium heat for a short period. In broiling, grilling or sautéing, when the juices run clear, it is done. Liver is at its best if still pink in the center.

LIVER DUMPLINGS

1/4 pound liver (any kind), minced
1 tablespoon butter
1 tablespoon finely chopped parsley
1 tablespoon finely chopped green onions
1/2 teaspoon salt
1/4 teaspoon freshly ground pepper
1/4 teaspoon freshly grated nutmeg
1 egg, beaten
1/3 to 1/2 cup bread crumbs

Combine all ingredients, adding just enough bread crumbs for mixture to hold its shape. Poach dumplings in salted water for 10 to 15 minutes; drain and cool. Then fry until golden in deep hot oil. Serve with sauerkraut or cabbage for an entrée or on toothpicks for an appetizer. Pass Pommery or Dijon-style mustard.
Makes 2 dozen 1-inch dumplings

Variation: Drop dumplings into 2 quarts simmering rich homemade chicken stock to which diced carrot and celeriac have been added. Cook for about 15 minutes and serve dumplings with the soup.

CHICKEN LIVER ROLL-UPS

5 chicken livers, cut in half
1 large eggplant, unpeeled
salt
2 tablespoons butter
1 clove garlic, finely chopped
1 onion, thinly sliced
2 tablespoons olive oil
salt and freshly ground pepper
vegetable oil for deep-frying
hot tomato salsa (see Basics)

Cut eggplant in 10 slices, sprinkle with salt and set aside for 10 minutes. Then squeeze out liquid and pat dry. Heat butter with garlic and sauté onions until transparent; add oil and the livers and sauté quickly. Season to taste with salt and pepper. Place a piece of liver on each eggplant slice, roll up and fasten with a toothpick. Fry in deep hot oil until golden. Serve as a first course with fresh tomato sauce. Also makes a nice supper dish served with almond pilaf.
Serves 8 as a first course; 4 to 6 as a main dish

CHOPPED LIVER

What Jewish household is unfamiliar with this dish? If you want to prepare liver in the traditional kosher style, first rinse liver well in cold water, drain and sprinkle coarse salt over its entire surface. Broil to draw out blood. Wash carefully and proceed with following recipe. (This preparation applies only to beef or veal liver.)

1 pound chicken, beef or veal liver
2 tablespoons rendered chicken fat
   or margarine
1 large onion, chopped
2 to 4 hard-cooked eggs, chopped
salt and freshly ground pepper
dash of cayenne (optional)
chicken stock as needed

Sauté onions in chicken fat until transparent, add liver and brown on all sides. Remove liver and chop well. Add eggs and season with salt and pepper to taste. If too dry, add a little chicken stock.

Variations: Follow the preceding recipe, substituting sweet butter for the chicken fat and add the following ingredients: 2 tablespoons chopped chives and 2 tablespoons chopped parsley; or 1/2 cup chopped shallots which have been sautéed in 1 tablespoon butter; or 1 teaspoon chopped fresh tarragon; or 1 teaspoon anchovy paste; or Cognac or dry sherry instead of the chicken stock.

RUMAKI

8 chicken livers, cut in thirds
24 whole water chestnuts
12 slices bacon, cut in half
1/4 cup soy sauce
1/2 teaspoon curry powder
1/2 teaspoon freshly grated ginger root

Combine a chicken liver third with a water chestnut and wrap a piece of bacon around it; fasten with a toothpick. Repeat using all livers, water chestnuts and bacon. Combine soy sauce, curry powder and ginger in a bowl. Marinate rumakis in this mixture for 1 hour. Drain, and broil, grill or deep-fry, turning frequently, until bacon is crisp.
Makes 24 rumakis

LIVER KNISHES

Filling:

1/2 pound cooked meat or poultry
   (use leftovers)
1/2 pound boiled or broiled calf liver,
   cooked just until tender
1 onion, chopped
1 stalk celery, chopped
1 bell pepper, chopped
2 tablespoons rendered chicken fat
1 teaspoon salt
1/4 teaspoon freshly ground pepper

Dough:

2 pounds potatoes
3 eggs, beaten
1/3 cup rendered chicken fat
1 teaspoon salt
2 cups flour
3 tablespoons rendered chicken fat
   (for baking)

To make filling, lightly sauté onion, celery and bell pepper in fat. Put through meat grinder together with the meat and livers. Season to taste. Set aside.

To make dough, boil potatoes, skin and mash well; add eggs, fat and salt; mix well. Place 1 cup flour in the corner of a pastry board; spoon potato mixture over flour, allowing it to absorb enough flour to make it workable. Dust board with remaining flour. Flatten dough, making a 4x8-inch rectangle; spread filling down center of it, fold in half lengthwise and pinch edges together. Roll carefully with floured fingers from center, doubling length. Cut in 1-inch pieces. Heat 3 tablespoons chicken fat in baking dish, fill with knishes and bake in a 400° oven for 30 minutes. Turn knishes and return to oven for another 10 to 15 minutes until knishes are golden brown. Serve as appetizer or side dish. Makes 16 knishes

MATZO LIVER PANCAKES

1/2 cup finely chopped cooked
   chicken or calf liver
2 eggs, separated
1 tablespoon sugar
1 teaspoon salt
1/2 cup matzo meal
1/2 cup chicken stock
1/2 teaspoon curry powder (optional)
1 small onion, finely chopped

Beat egg whites, gradually adding sugar and salt. Lightly beat yolks and fold egg whites into them. Then gently stir in liver and all other ingredients. Use 2 to 3 tablespoons batter for each pancake. Fry on a hot greased griddle. Serve with applesauce.
Makes 8 pancakes

LIVER PUDDING

This is a Scandinavian preparation for liver. Most often it is sliced and served for breakfast or brunch.

3/4 pound liver, minced (any kind)
2 tablespoons butter
1 onion, finely chopped
2 cups cooked rice
1/2 cup raisins
3 eggs, beaten
1/4 teaspoon marjoram
1 teaspoon salt
1/4 cup honey or syrup
2 cups milk
lingonberry or cranberry jelly

Heat butter in skillet and sauté onions until transparent; remove from heat and add rice. Add liver and raisins. Then combine with remaining ingredients, except jelly, and stir well. Pour batter into a buttered 2-quart casserole. Dot with butter. Bake, uncovered, in a 350° oven for 40 to 45 minutes. Serve with lingonberry or cranberry jelly.
Serves 8

CALF LIVER BABAS

This is a rather spectacular way of presenting liver to your luncheon guests. It also makes a lovely first course.

1/2 pound finely ground calf liver
1 tablespoon butter
1 tablespoon flour
3/4 cup milk
1/2 teaspoon salt
1/4 teaspoon white pepper
1/8 teaspoon freshly grated nutmeg
dash of marjoram
1 whole egg, slightly beaten
1 egg yolk
Béarnaise sauce (see Basics)

Melt butter in saucepan and blend in flour to make a paste. Slowly add milk over low heat and stir until thickened. Add seasonings. Remove from heat and blend in egg and egg yolk. Add liver, mix well and press through a fine sieve or purée in blender until smooth. Fill small buttered baba molds two-thirds full. Bake in a pan of hot water in a 350° oven until set, about 15 to 25 minutes, depending on size of mold. Unmold and serve with Béarnaise sauce.
Serves 6 to 8, depending on baba mold

TOMATOES STUFFED WITH LIVER

8 tomatoes
1/2 pound liver (any kind)
1/2 cup soft bread crumbs
2 tablespoons chopped green onions
2 tablespoons milk
salt and freshly ground pepper to taste
2 eggs, beaten
2 tablespoons butter
1/2 cup sour cream

Select tomatoes of equal size. Cut slice from top and hollow out tomatoes, reserving pulp. Chop liver very fine and combine with bread crumbs, onions, milk, salt and pepper. Add eggs and mix well. Sauté the chopped liver mixture in butter for about 10 minutes, then stuff into tomatoes and cover with lids. Bake in a 350° oven for 35 minutes. Spoon sour cream over tomatoes and bake an additional 5 minutes.
Serves 4

Variation: This same mixture may be stuffed into mushrooms (omit sour cream), bell peppers, cabbage leaves or pastry.

LIVER

LIVER SAUTÉ

This recipe may be adapted to many varieties of liver, from calf or beef liver to pork, lamb or game liver. It might be noted that deer liver is considered the most delicate of all, and is especially delicious. Further, it is our opinion that liver should be grilled or sautéed medium rare—the center should still be pink.

1-1/2 pounds liver, membranes
    removed and sliced 1/2 inch thick
flour
3 tablespoons butter
3 tablespoons vegetable oil
salt and freshly ground pepper

Lightly dust liver slices with flour. Heat butter and oil in skillet and quickly brown the liver on both sides. Do not crowd in pan; do not overcook. Transfer liver to heated platter. Salt and pepper to taste. Serve with lemon wedges if desired.
Serves 4

For liver and bacon: Place 1/2 pound bacon slices in skillet and cook until crisp; drain on paper towels. Sauté liver slices in 6 tablespoons bacon fat, following directions above. Transfer to heated platter. Garnish with bacon and chopped parsley.

For liver and onions: Prepare liver as for liver sauté. Transfer to heated platter. Have ready 2 onions, thinly sliced. Add another tablespoon of butter and oil to skillet and sauté onions until golden. Then add 1/2 teaspoon Worcestershire sauce, 1/4 teaspoon Tabasco sauce and 1/4 cup dry red wine. Bring to a rapid boil, adjust seasonings and pour over liver.

For liver and mushrooms: Prepare liver as for liver sauté. Transfer to heated platter. Have ready 1/2 pound sliced mushrooms. Add 3 more tablespoons butter to skillet and sauté mushrooms over medium heat for 5 minutes. Then add 1/2 teaspoon tarragon, 1 teaspoon chives and 1/4 cup dry white wine. Bring to a rapid boil, adjust seasonings and immediately pour over liver.

GRILLED LIVER & APPLE FRITTERS

4 slices liver
8 1/2-inch onion rings
8 apple rings
beer batter (following)
oil for deep-frying

Prepare liver as for liver sauté (preceding). Transfer to heated platter. In the meantime, prepare beer batter. Then dip onion and apple rings into batter and fry in deep hot oil until golden. Pile on top of liver and serve.
Serves 4

BEER BATTER

1 cup beer
2 eggs, beaten
1 cup flour
pinch of salt

Beat beer into eggs. Then gradually add flour and salt, beating all the while. Use for apple and onion rings.

Sautéed chicken livers are a favorite breakfast specialty in many countries. The Mexicans serve theirs with tortillas and maybe some cinnamon-flavored orange slices. The Germans might make up potato pancakes to go along with theirs. Use your imagination. The following are two recipes for breakfast sautés.

MEXICAN CHICKEN LIVERS

1 pound chicken livers
flour seasoned with salt and pepper
1/2 cup chopped green onions
1/2 pound mushrooms, sliced
4 tablespoons butter
1/4 cup Madeira or sherry

Dust livers with seasoned flour. Sauté onions and mushrooms in butter until lightly browned. Add livers and sauté for 10 minutes. Add Madeira and simmer for 5 minutes to allow flavors to blend. Serve with hot tomato salsa (see Basics).
Serves 4

CHICKEN LIVER SAUTÉ, HUNGARIAN STYLE

1 pound chicken livers, halved, and dusted with
1 tablespoon flour
2 onions, sliced
3 tablespoons vegetable oil or butter
2 mild or hot green chilis, seeded and chopped
3 tomatoes, peeled and chopped
salt and freshly ground pepper to taste

Sauté onions in 2 tablespoons of the oil until transparent. Add livers and sauté about 5 minutes; remove to side. Add remaining oil to pan; add peppers and tomatoes and cook over medium heat for 10 minutes. Adjust seasonings with salt and pepper. Add chicken livers and onions that were set aside; continue cooking another 10 minutes. Good served over an omelette.
Serves 4

BASQUE CHICKEN LIVER SAUTÉ

1 pound chicken livers, dusted with
1 tablespoon flour
2 tablespoons olive oil
2 tablespoons butter
1 clove garlic, finely chopped
1/2 cup sliced mushrooms
1/2 cup dry white wine
1 tablespoon chopped parsley
salt and freshly ground pepper

Heat oil with garlic and sauté livers until browned. Add butter and mushrooms and sauté quickly. Add wine, parsley and seasonings. Cover and simmer for 3 minutes. Serve with saffron rice or wild rice.
Serves 4

CRISP-FRIED CHICKEN LIVERS

1 pound chicken livers, cut in half
1 tablespoon soy sauce
1 tablespoon dry sherry
1 teaspoon finely minced fresh
 ginger root
1 clove garlic, finely chopped
2 tablespoons minced green onions
1/2 cup flour
2 tablespoons cornstarch
peanut oil for deep-frying

Marinate chicken livers in mixture of soy sauce, sherry, ginger, garlic and green onions for 1 hour. Then add flour and cornstarch, mixing only to blend. Drop the chicken livers, one at a time, in deep, hot oil and fry for 3 to 5 minutes until brown, crispy and cooked through but not dry. These make wonderful appetizers served with hot mustard, catsup or soy.
Serves 4

Variation: Gizzards and hearts may be prepared as above. Cut gizzards in half to separate 2 sections; score in criss-cross manner to allow for even cooking. Gizzards require 1 or 2 minutes longer cooking time than livers or hearts.

CURRIED LIVER

1-1/2 pounds lamb, calf or chicken
 livers
2 onions, thinly sliced
2 cloves garlic, finely chopped
2 tablespoons each butter and
 vegetable oil
1 or more dried red chilis, minced
1/2 teaspoon freshly grated ginger root
1 tablespoon minced coriander
1/4 teaspoon cumin
1/2 teaspoon turmeric
1/2 teaspoon cracked black pepper
1 teaspoon salt
1 cup coconut milk

Remove membranes from liver and cut in 1-inch pieces. (If using chicken livers, cut them in half.) Sauté onions and garlic in butter and oil until transparent. Add chili, spices and seasonings; continue sautéing for 2 minutes longer. Add liver and sauté 3 more minutes. Stir in coconut milk; simmer, uncovered, for 8 to 10 minutes, or just until liver is cooked. Serve over plain rice or a saffron-flavored rice with condiments such as chutney, sieved egg yolk and chopped egg whites (prepared separately by tradition), toasted coconut, chopped peanuts, chopped green onions, cucumbers and raisins.
Serves 4 to 6

SWEET & SOUR CHICKEN LIVERS WITH PINEAPPLE

1 pound chicken livers
1 cup pineapple juice (or part water)
2 tablespoons vinegar
2 tablespoons sugar
2 tablespoons catsup
2 tablespoons cornstarch
1 cup pineapple chunks
1 bell pepper, cut in 1-inch chunks
1 Bermuda onion, cut in 1-inch chunks
1 tablespoon toasted sesame seeds

Prepare livers in same manner as preceding recipe for crisp-fried chicken livers; keep warm. To make sauce, mix together pineapple juice, vinegar, sugar, catsup and cornstarch. Cook over medium heat, stirring constantly, until mixture comes almost to the boil and is slightly thickened. Add pineapple, bell pepper and onion; again bring just to the boil. Pour over chicken livers and sprinkle with toasted sesame seeds. Serve with rice.
Serves 4

CORNISH GAME HEN STUFFED WITH CHICKEN LIVERS

4 Cornish game hens
3/4 pound chicken livers, cut in half
1 cup chopped fresh mushrooms
1/4 cup ham, cut in thin strips
1/4 cup pistachios or pine nuts
2 tablespoons butter
salt and freshly ground pepper
juice of 1/2 lemon
bacon strips

Sauté chicken livers, mushrooms, ham and nuts in butter. Stuff mixture loosely into birds. Truss with white string or skewers. Rub birds with salt, pepper and lemon juice. Place a couple strips of bacon over the birds and roast 45 minutes to 1 hour in a 350° oven. Serves 4

Variation: This stuffing may also be used for squab or any other small bird.

CHICKEN LIVERS & SPAGHETTI

1 pound chicken livers, quartered
flour seasoned with salt and pepper
1 clove garlic, finely chopped
2 onions, chopped
4 tablespoons olive oil
2-1/2 cups peeled, seeded tomatoes, put through sieve
1 6-ounce can tomato paste
1 tablespoon chopped fresh basil
1 sprig rosemary
1/2 teaspoon crushed oregano
1/4 teaspoon cinnamon
salt and cayenne to taste
1/2 cup dry red wine
1/2 pound spaghetti or green noodles
freshly grated Parmesan cheese

Sauté garlic and onions in 2 tablespoons of the olive oil. Add tomatoes, tomato paste, seasonings and wine. Simmer for about 1 hour, stirring from time to time, until smooth and slightly thickened.

Lightly dust chicken livers with seasoned flour and sauté in remaining 2 tablespoons oil. Add to sauce and cook for 10 minutes.

In the meantime, cook spaghetti or noodles al dente; drain and put on heated platter. Pour chicken liver sauce over all and serve with freshly grated Parmesan cheese, crusty bread and a green salad.

Serves 4 to 6

LIVER

TUSCAN MIXED GRILL

6 small slices pork loin
6 small pieces boned chicken
6 slices pork liver
6 small rib lamb chops, or
6 pieces lean lamb stew meat
12 slices lean bacon, halved
24 leaves fresh sage
2 sprigs rosemary, ground in a mortar
freshly ground pepper
1/2 cup olive oil
3 to 4 juniper berries, crushed, or
1/2 teaspoon fennel seeds, bruised
salt to taste

Skewer pork, chicken, liver and lamb, placing a bacon strip and sage leaf between each. Sprinkle with rosemary and freshly ground pepper to taste.
Place skewers, side by side in a shallow baking dish and pour olive oil over them. Add the juniper berries and marinate 3 to 4 hours. Grill over charcoal, turning frequently, about 15 minutes; sprinkle with salt. Or, place on a rack in a baking pan and roast in a 450° oven for about the same time. Serve with a raisin pilaf.
Serves 6

SOUR PORK LIVER

1 pork liver, membranes removed
   and cut in strips
1 onion, chopped
4 slices bacon, diced
1 tablespoon flour
1/2 cup chicken stock
1/4 cup lemon juice
salt and freshly ground pepper to taste

Fry onion and bacon together for 5 minutes. Then add liver and sauté another 2 minutes over high heat. Transfer to heated platter. Add flour to pan and stir well. Gradually add stock and bring to boil, cooking for 5 minutes. Add lemon juice; adjust seasonings. Pour sauce over liver. Serve immediately.
Serves 4

LIVER PAPRIKA

1-1/2 pounds calf or lamb liver,
   cut in 1-inch cubes
3 tablespoons flour
1 tablespoon paprika
1/2 teaspoon salt
1/2 teaspoon freshly ground pepper
1/4 cup olive oil
1 onion, thinly sliced
1/4 cup chopped parsley
1/2 pint sour cream

Remove membranes from liver. Then combine flour with paprika, salt and pepper and sprinkle on liver. Heat 3 tablespoons of the oil in skillet and sauté liver cubes until brown, about 3 to 5 minutes. Transfer to heated platter. Add another tablespoon oil to the skillet and sauté onions and parsley until onions are transparent. Add sour cream and heat without boiling so as not to curdle sour cream. Pour over liver and serve immediately. Serve with buttered noodles or boiled potatoes.
Serves 4

Variation: Chicken livers, halved, may be substituted in this recipe.

LIVER & VEGETABLE STIR-FRY

1 pound liver (any kind)
1 tablespoon hoisin sauce* or
    soy sauce
2 tablespoons dry sherry
1 teaspoon sugar
1/2 teaspoon fried sesame oil**
2 stalks celery, cut in 1/4-inch
    diagonal slices
1 cup sliced bamboo shoots
1/2 pound sugar peas (Chinese pea
    pods)
1/4 pound button mushrooms,
    left whole
salt to taste
1/2 cup chicken stock
1 tablespoon cornstarch
peanut oil for stir-frying

Cut liver in 1/4x1-inch-thick slices, or cut chicken livers into thirds. Combine hoisin, sherry, sugar and sesame oil in a bowl and marinate liver for 30 minutes. Heat 2 tablespoons oil in wok and add celery, bamboo shoots, sugar peas and mushrooms; salt lightly and stir-fry for 2 minutes. Add stock,
cover and let steam rise to top (about 1 minute). Do not overcook. Remove vegetables to heated dish; keep warm. Quickly return wok to heat and add 3 tablespoons oil. Sprinkle livers with cornstarch and stir lightly. Add livers to very hot wok and stir-fry about 1-1/2 minutes to brown. Place on top of vegetables and serve immediately with hot rice.
Serves 4
  *Available in Oriental markets
**The dark seasoning oil available in Oriental markets.

BAKED CALF LIVER

1 whole calf liver (about 1-1/2 pounds)
vegetable oil
1/2 cup vinegar
1 onion, sliced
4 sprigs parsley
1 sprig thyme
salt and freshly ground pepper to taste
4 slices bacon

Brush liver with oil. Combine vinegar, onion, parsley, thyme, salt and pepper and marinate liver for 24 hours in the refrigerator. Remove from refrigerator and let stand 1 hour before roasting. Place in a roasting pan and top with bacon, then onion slices from marinade. Put in a 375° oven for 25 to 30 minutes, basting from time to time.
Serves 6

STUFFED CALF LIVER

1 2-pound piece calf liver
1/4 pound bacon, diced
1 onion, chopped
1/2 cup bread crumbs
2 tablespoons minced parsley
1 egg, beaten
1/2 cup sour cream
salt and freshly ground pepper to taste
1/4 cup vegetable oil

Make a slash through center of liver to form pocket. Place bacon, onion, bread crumbs and parsley in skillet and fry until onions are transparent; cool. Combine bacon mixture with egg and sour cream and season with salt and pepper. Put mixture into liver pocket and truss with white string or skewers. Place in a shallow baking dish and rub well with oil. Bake in a 350° oven for about 1 hour. Slice liver and pour any pan juices over it. Serve with brown rice or dumplings.
Serves 6 to 8

KIDNEYS

Men of Paleolithic times killed their prey, carved up the flesh for transport home, then rewarded themselves with a banquet of the more perishable parts—kidneys, liver, brains, heart, the fat behind the eyeballs and the soft internal organs. Kidneys have played an important role in man's diet ever since. Generally regarded as one of the most nourishing of all foods, kidneys have been eaten by the peoples of practically every culture, and especially by the Chinese (pork), Middle Easterners (lamb), Spanish (veal) and English (veal and beef).

Animal kidneys have been found among the relics evacuated from Egyptian tombs of the 12th century B.C. Though the Egyptian peasant diet consisted mainly of beer, bread and onions, the rich feasted upon the kidneys and flesh of antelopes and gazelles. In later times, in the courts of the caliphs about the 10th century A.D., kidneys of kid were strung beside the carcass of the animal, delicately flavored with mint and lemon juice and roasted over an open fire. Kidneys were popular at medieval banquets, being included in such dishes as meat pies and pasties. This might have been a forerunner to the traditional British beef and kidney pie.

Kidneys did pass through a period of rejection during the Italian Renaissance. The people generally believed they were responsible for man's bad humors. (The heart, liver and spleen were also condemned.) However, their unpopularity was short-lived, as the chefs of 18th and 19th century France and England rediscovered them and used them extravagantly. Within the volume of *The Compleat Housewife*, printed in England in 1727, one can find many dishes using kidneys—everyday dishes as well as more elaborate hot hors d'oeuvre.

Kidneys are also valued because of the fat that encases them. Called suet, or leaf fat, it is considered the finest of all fat. It makes marvelous pastry for beef or other pot pies and should be used exclusively in English plum pudding or mincemeat. Suet was also one of the ingredients (along with cows' udders and warm milk) used in the first margarine, invented by a French food technologist in the late 1860's.

PREPARATION OF KIDNEYS

It is curious that kidneys have taken on different shapes within the bodies of various quadrupeds. Beef or veal kidneys are multi-lobed and elongated, while the kidneys of lamb and pork have a single lobe that is bean-shaped. Many people object to beef and pork kidneys because of their strong odor. However, if they are properly cleaned and soaked, the objectionable odor dissipates. A perfectly cooked kidney is a sign of a good chef. Keep in mind that kidneys must be grilled or sautéed quickly to be tender. Overcooking toughens, thereby requiring long, slow cooking to make them tender again.

Step I: Cleaning
Remove outside membrane from all kidneys with a sharp, pointed knife. Split beef or pork kidneys in half lengthwise and remove white core and excess fat from center with a sharp knife; this is not necessary for lamb or veal kidneys. Any fat surrounding the kidney should be reserved for later use; this is true suet, the best of all fat.

Step II: Soaking
Beef and pork kidneys should be soaked in acidulated water (1 tablespoon lemon juice or vinegar to 2 cups water) or buttermilk for 1 hour. Never soak veal or lamb kidneys as they have a tendency to soak up too much water due to their more delicate flavor and texture. (Baby beef kidneys, sold under the guise of veal, often require soaking because once the calf is weaned, the inner core becomes stronger.) Drain and pat dry before proceeding with recipe (unless parboiling is to follow). Additionally, baking soda or salt may be rubbed into beef or pork kidneys to further remove any pungent odor. Rinse well.

Step III: Parboiling
Parboil pork or beef kidneys just 1 minute to remove excess blood and clinging parts. Add 1 tablespoon lemon juice to the water, if desired. Do not overcook. This is especially recommended in many of the Chinese recipes as it makes the juice clearer when stir-frying.

PORK KIDNEYS
IN WHISKEY SOUP

This is a very clever way of eating your whiskey. The Chinese found this out centuries ago when they first combined two "warming" ingredients— fresh ginger and strong rice wine. It's a perfect way to ward off the chill of a cold winter's evening.

1-1/2 pounds pork kidneys
2 tablespoons peanut oil
1/4 cup thinly sliced fresh ginger root
1 tablespoon soy sauce
1 teaspoon salt
1/2 cup whiskey

Prepare kidneys according to Steps I and II in basic instructions, splitting and cleaning kidneys before soaking. Then parboil in salted water (1 teaspoon salt to 1 quart water) for 1 minute; drain. Heat oil in a pot and when it just begins to smoke, add kidneys and ginger and stir-fry for a minute. Then add soy, salt and 2 tablespoons of the whiskey. Brown slightly before adding remaining whiskey and 1-1/2 quarts water. Bring just to a boil, reduce heat and simmer for 10 minutes. Serve immediately in soup bowls. Serves 4 to 6

SOUP WITH KIDNEY DUMPLINGS

1 veal kidney
1 tablespoon butter
1 tablespoon beef marrow (scraped from a 3-inch marrow bone)
1/2 cup white bread crumbs
1 tablespoon flour
1 tablespoon finely chopped parsley
salt and freshly ground pepper to taste
3 egg yolks, beaten
2 quarts beef stock

Remove any fat or membrane from kidney according to Step I in basic instructions; pat dry and finely chop. Melt butter in a skillet and cook kidneys and marrow for 5 minutes. Put mixture into a bowl. Add bread crumbs, flour, parsley, salt and pepper. Bind all with egg yolks. Mixture should be firm (more flour might be necessary). Mold into 3/4-inch balls. Bring stock to a simmer and drop dumplings into stock. Cook 10 minutes. Serve in soup tureen or in individual bowls.
Serves 6

GRILLED KIDNEYS

Keep kidneys in large pieces if possible; lamb and veal kidneys are actually nice grilled whole. If split, skewer flat with toothpicks to keep edges from rolling up; this is not necessary if smaller pieces or cubes are used. Spread cut side of kidney with melted butter and sprinkle with fine bread crumbs and set on grill, cut side up. Cook for several minutes. Turn over, brush again with melted butter, sprinkle with more bread crumbs and grill a minute or 2 longer. Serve with lemon wedges, crisp bacon and French fries or boiled potatoes. Or serve on toast or a bed of risotto or pilaf.

Variation: Blend butter with herbs such as parsley, tarragon, chives, shallots, or prepared Dijon-style mustard or lemon juice.

Variation: Skewer kidneys alternately with squares of parboiled salt pork or bacon and sautéed mushroom caps.

SKEWERED KIDNEYS

12 lamb or veal kidneys
1/2 cup olive oil
salt and freshly ground pepper to taste
1/4 teaspoon thyme
1/4 teaspoon dry mustard
1/4 teaspoon mace
dash of cayenne

Prepare kidneys according to Step I in basic instructions. Split lengthwise and thread each piece on a wooden skewer. Place in a shallow pan, cut side up.
Make a marinade by combining remaining ingredients and pour over kidneys. Marinate 10 minutes, turning frequently. Drain. Place skewered kidneys cut side down on broiler rack or barbecue grill. Broil 4 to 5 minutes on first side; turn and broil about 3 minutes longer.
Serves 4 to 6

Variation: Follow above recipe, but thread marinated kidneys on skewers along with whole mushrooms, parboiled pearl onions and bacon squares.

KIDNEYS IN THEIR OVERCOATS

This is a traditional Irish dish that is often served for breakfast. It would be good served with hash browns and scrambled eggs. For lunch, serve on dry toast accompanied by boiled potatoes in their jackets and braised fresh spinach or cabbage.

Ask the butcher to leave on the outer layer of fat (called leaf fat) that surrounds the kidneys. This fat gets wonderfully crispy in cooking, at the same time preventing overcooking and loss of juices. Allow 2 to 3 lamb kidneys (veal kidneys would be good, too) per person. Place in a shallow baking dish in a preheated 400° oven for 30 minutes, or until fat is melted and crispy. Split open on dry toast; salt and pepper to taste.

KIDNEYS IN RED WINE

1 pound kidneys (any kind)
4 tablespoons or more butter
1 onion, chopped
1 cup sliced mushrooms
1/2 teaspoon tarragon
1 tablespoon chopped parsley
1/2 cup dry red wine
1/4 cup beef stock
salt and freshly ground pepper to taste

Prepare kidneys according to Steps I and II (if pork or beef) in basic instructions. Drain and slice in bite-size pieces. Heat butter in skillet and sauté kidneys over high heat; remove and keep warm. Add onion, mushrooms, tarragon and parsley to pan, sautéing until onions are transparent. Deglaze pan with wine and stock; bring to a boil. Return kidneys to pan, season with salt and pepper and cook several minutes until very hot. Serve on dry toast or over fluffy rice.
Serves 4

VEAL KIDNEYS WITH MADEIRA & SOUR CREAM

4 veal kidneys
flour
2 tablespoons each butter and
    vegetable oil
1/2 cup Madeira
2 tablespoons chopped chives
1/4 cup sour cream
salt and freshly ground pepper
dash of cayenne

Prepare kidneys according to Step I in basic instructions and thinly slice. Dust with flour and sauté quickly in hot butter and oil until golden. Remove to a warm platter; keep warm. Deglaze pan with Madeira; add chives. Reduce heat and add sour cream, stirring all the while; do not boil. Season with salt, pepper and cayenne. Pour sauce over kidneys.
Serves 4

VEAL KIDNEYS IN WHITE WINE

4 veal kidneys, or
8 lamb kidneys
2 tablespoons olive oil
3 tablespoons butter
2 tablespoons chopped parsley
1 tablespoon finely chopped shallots
2 tablespoons flour
1-1/2 cups dry white wine
1/2 cup chicken or beef stock
1 tablespoon lemon juice
salt and freshly ground pepper to taste

Prepare kidneys according to Step I in basic instructions; cut into 1-inch slices. Heat olive oil and 2 tablespoons butter in skillet; add kidneys and sauté on both sides. Reduce heat and add parsley and shallots. Cook several minutes; remove to warm dish and keep warm. Add flour to skillet; then deglaze with wine and stock, stirring constantly, until smooth and thickened. Remove from heat and add 1 tablespoon butter, lemon juice, salt and pepper. Pour over kidneys.
Serves 4

SAUTÉED KIDNEYS ANDALUSIA

4 veal kidneys
6 tablespoons olive oil
1/2 cup chopped ham (prosciutto
  or Virginia ham preferred)
1 cup finely chopped onions
2 cloves garlic, finely chopped
1 small bay leaf
1 tablespoon flour
1/2 cup chicken stock
2 tablespoons finely chopped parsley
1/2 cup pale dry sherry
salt and freshly ground pepper to taste

Prepare kidneys according to Step I in basic instructions. Split in half lengthwise; then cut into 1-inch slices. Heat 4 tablespoons olive oil in skillet over high heat. Add ham, onions, garlic and bay leaf. Reduce heat slightly and sauté until onions are transparent. Add flour and mix thoroughly. Add stock and cook, stirring constantly, until mixture is smooth and thickened. Add parsley; reduce heat and cook 3 minutes longer.
Heat remaining oil in another skillet. Add kidneys and sauté quickly on both sides. Transfer kidneys to plate. Deglaze pan with sherry; bring to a boil. Return kidneys to pan along with onion sauce. Heat through; adjust seasonings with salt and pepper.
Serves 6

VEAL KIDNEYS BORDELAISE

6 veal kidneys
salt and freshly ground pepper to taste
5 tablespoons butter
1/4 cup finely chopped shallots
1/2 cup dry red wine
2 tablespoons flour
1-1/2 cups rich beef stock
2 tablespoons tomato paste
pinch of thyme
1 teaspoon lemon juice
2 tablespoons chopped beef marrow
1 tablespoon chopped parsley

Prepare kidneys according to Step I in basic instructions; cut into 1-inch slices. Season well with salt and pepper. Heat butter in skillet and sauté kidneys quickly over high heat. Transfer to flameproof casserole. Add shallots to skillet and sauté until transparent. Add wine and reduce to 3 tablespoons over high heat. Combine flour with 1 cup of the stock and blend well. Add this mixture along with remaining stock, tomato paste, thyme, lemon juice, marrow and parsley to skillet, blending well; cook until thickened. Pour all the sauce over the kidneys and heat just until simmering.
Serves 6

VEAL KIDNEYS FLAMBÉ

6 veal kidneys
4 tablespoons butter
1 tablespoon minced shallots
18 mushroom caps
2 tablespoons Cognac, warmed
1/4 cup dry sherry
2 to 3 tablespoons heavy cream
salt and freshly ground pepper to taste
watercress or chopped parsley
   for garnish

Remove membrane from kidneys according to Step I in basic instructions; do not wash or soak. Slice crosswise in 1/4-inch slices. Heat butter in sauté pan; add shallots and sauté until transparent. Add mushrooms and kidneys and cook until lightly browned. Pour warmed Cognac over all and ignite. When flame dies down, add sherry. Simmer gently 1 or 2 minutes to reduce slightly. Stir in cream; adjust seasonings with salt and pepper. Allow sauce to thicken slightly. Garnish with watercress or parsley; serve with rice.
Serves 6

SAUTÉED PORK KIDNEYS

4 pork kidneys, about 1 pound
buttermilk
3 tablespoons bacon fat
1 onion, chopped
1 cup sliced apples with skin
1/2 teaspoon caraway seeds
1/2 teaspoon freshly ground pepper
1 teaspoon flour
beef stock as needed

Soak and clean kidneys according to Steps I and II in basic instructions, using buttermilk in soaking liquid. Rinse, pat dry and cut into slices. Heat fat in a large skillet and sauté onion until transparent. Add kidneys and brown on both sides, about 2 minutes. Add apples, caraway seeds and pepper and continue cooking over medium-high heat for about 8 minutes. Then sprinkle with flour, add a little stock and cook until slightly thickened. Serve with sauerkraut, potatoes and black bread.
Serves 4

VEAL & KIDNEY SAUTÉ

2 veal kidneys
1 pound veal cutlets, cut
   1/4 inch thick
1/2 teaspoon salt
1/4 teaspoon freshly ground pepper
4 or more tablespoons butter
1 cup mushroom caps
1/4 cup dry sherry
1-1/2 cups cooked vegetables, either
   julienne carrots and string beans,
   or lima beans and pearl onions

Clean, pat dry and slice kidneys into bite-size pieces. Season veal with salt and pepper. Heat 3 tablespoons butter in skillet and sauté veal on both sides; place on warm platter and keep warm. Add remaining butter, kidneys and mushrooms and sauté until kidneys are tender. Remove to platter and keep warm. Deglaze pan with sherry and bring to a boil; adjust seasonings and pour over meat. Garnish platter with cooked vegetables.
Serves 4

PORK KIDNEY SAUTÉ WITH PILAF

6 pork kidneys
4 or more tablespoons butter
1 onion, chopped
1/4 cup chopped parsley
1-1/2 cups white or brown rice
2-3/4 cups beef stock, heated to
    boiling point
1/4 cup slivered, blanched almonds
1 tablespoon olive oil
1/2 cup dry white wine
salt and freshly ground pepper to taste
dash of cayenne

Prepare kidneys according to Steps I and II in basic instructions; slice. Continue with Step III. Heat butter in a 1-1/2-quart saucepan; add onion, parsley and rice and cook until lightly browned. Add stock, cover and simmer until liquid has evaporated and rice is cooked through (20 to 30 minutes for white rice, 30 to 40 minutes for brown rice).

In the meantime, sauté almonds in oil until golden. Remove from pan; set aside. Add a little butter if necessary to the same pan; add kidneys and sauté 4 to 5 minutes. Set aside and keep warm. Deglaze pan with wine, add seasonings and reduce to half. Return kidneys to pan and heat through. Pile cooked rice on serving platter in a ring, place sautéed kidneys in the center and garnish with almonds.
Serves 6

VEAL SCHNITZEL WITH KIDNEYS

2 veal kidneys
1 pound veal cutlets, pounded
    1/4 inch thick
flour for dredging
6 tablespoons butter
8 large mushroom caps
1/3 cup beef stock
1/3 cup dry sherry
1/4 teaspoon freshly grated nutmeg
1/4 teaspoon paprika
salt and freshly ground pepper to taste

Prepare kidneys according to Step I in basic instructions; cut each kidney into 8 slices. Dredge cutlets with flour. Heat 4 tablespoons butter in a skillet. Add the cutlets and brown on both sides; remove and keep warm. Add remaining butter, kidneys and mushrooms; sauté quickly over high heat, 1 or 2 minutes. Top cutlets with kidneys and mushrooms. Keep warm. Deglaze pan with stock and sherry. Add nutmeg, paprika, salt and pepper. Bring to boil and reduce by half; pour over meat. Serve hot with boiled potatoes and glazed carrots.
Serves 4

Variations: Follow the above recipe, substituting 1/2 pound chicken livers for the veal kidneys. Or follow the above recipe, substituting boned chicken breasts for the veal cutlets. Either veal kidneys or 1/2 pound chicken livers may be used with the chicken breasts.

KIDNEY, TOMATO & BELL PEPPER STIR-FRY

1 pound beef or pork kidneys
2 tablespoons peanut oil
2 thin slices fresh ginger root,
    finely chopped
1 clove garlic, finely chopped
1 tablespoon soy sauce
2 tablespoons dry sherry
1 pound tomatoes, cut in wedges
1 bell pepper, cut in 1-inch pieces
1 onion, cut in 1-inch pieces
1 tablespoon sugar
1 teaspoon cornstarch, mixed with
1/4 cup water
salt to taste

Soak and clean kidneys according to Steps I and II in basic instructions; cut into 1-inch pieces. Then parboil pieces in salted water (1 teaspoon salt to 1 quart water) for 1 minute only; drain. Heat oil in skillet or wok over high heat; add the ginger and garlic and let sizzle 30 seconds. Add kidneys and stir-fry until lightly browned (another 30 seconds). Then add soy, sherry, tomatoes, bell pepper, onion and sugar. Cover and let steam rise to top and vegetables heat through, about 3 to 5 minutes. Bind juices with cornstarch mixture, stirring constantly. Adjust seasonings. Serve immediately with steamed rice.
Serves 4 to 6

Variations: Lamb or veal kidneys may be substituted for the beef or pork kidneys in the above recipe. Omit parboiling in this case. For a spicier version, follow the above recipe, adding 1 finely chopped dried red chili when adding the vegetables. For kidney and asparagus stir-fry, follow the above recipe, omitting the tomatoes and bell pepper. Substitute 1-1/2 pounds asparagus, sliced on the diagonal 1/4 inch thick, and 1/2 cup water. For kidney and broccoli stir-fry, follow above recipe, omitting the tomatoes and bell pepper. Substitute 1-1/2 pounds broccoli, cut in flowerets and 1/4 pound thinly sliced and chopped ham. Omit salt in this case.

KIDNEYS WITH JUNIPER BERRIES

2 pounds beef, pork or game kidneys
salt and freshly ground pepper to taste
4 tablespoons butter
1/2 cup dry red wine
4 juniper berries, crushed
1 teaspoon grated lemon peel

Soak and clean kidneys according to Steps I and II in basic instructions. Cut in bite-size pieces and sprinkle with salt and pepper. Heat butter and brown kidneys on both sides. Add wine and juniper berries, cover and cook 2 minutes. Uncover, reduce heat, and cook about 5 to 7 minutes longer, until kidneys are cooked through and juices are reduced by half. Stir in lemon peel at last minute. Adjust seasonings.
Serves 4 to 6

ROAST LEG OF VEAL & KIDNEYS

5-pound leg of veal, boned
2 veal kidneys, with their fat
1 tablespoon paprika
salt and freshly ground pepper to taste
4 tablespoons butter
1 cup chicken stock
1/4 cup heavy cream or sour cream

Lay boned veal flat. Sprinkle kidneys with paprika and place in center of veal; season with salt and pepper. Roll up veal tightly around kidneys and secure with string in several places. Preheat oven to 400°. Place butter in roasting pan and allow to melt. Place roast in pan and brown for 15 minutes, turning from time to time. Add the stock to the pan. Reduce temperature to 325°; continue roasting, uncovered, for 2 hours, or until done, basting frequently. Remove to warm platter. Thicken pan juices with cream; serve separately. Complete menu with parslied potatoes or egg noodles and boiled red cabbage.

Variation: Sprinkle veal with chopped fresh herbs such as parsley, shallots, chervil and chives before tying roast.

KIDNEY RAGOUT

1 pound beef kidney
4 tablespoons butter
1 onion, chopped
4 tablespoons flour
2 cups beef stock
1/4 cup dry red wine
1/4 cup tomato paste
salt and freshly ground pepper to taste
1 small sprig fresh thyme, or
1/4 teaspoon dried thyme

Soak and clean kidneys according to Steps I and II in basic instructions; drain and cut in thin slices. Heat butter in skillet and sauté kidneys and onions until kidneys are golden and onions are transparent; remove and set aside. Stir flour into pan and cook 3 to 4 minutes, scraping edges to remove clinging particles. Add stock, wine and tomato paste and cook until thickened. Add seasonings and kidneys and heat through. Serve over fluffy rice.
Serves 4

STEAK & KIDNEY PIE

3/4 pound veal, beef or lamb kidneys
1/4 cup kidney suet, finely chopped,
    or half butter and half suet
1 onion, chopped
1-1/2 pounds chuck or round steak,
    cut in 3/4-inch cubes
3 cups beef stock
1 teaspoon salt
1/2 teaspoon freshly ground pepper
1 tablespoon Worcestershire sauce
3 tablespoons flour
rich pastry for 2-crust pie (see Basics)

Prepare kidneys according to Steps I and II in basic instructions, depending on variety of kidneys used. Cut into 1/2-inch cubes and set aside. Heat suet in a large skillet until melted; add onion and sauté until transparent. Then add steak and brown; add stock, salt, pepper and Worcestershire sauce, cover, and simmer for 1 hour until meat is tender. Add kidneys. Thicken juices by sifting flour gradually into the pan, stirring all the while. Remove from heat and let cool. Line a 2-quart casserole with pastry and pour in cooled meat filling. Fit with pastry, prick top well and seal edges. Bake in a 425° oven for 1 hour, or until crust is golden.
Serves 6

Variation: Follow above recipe, adding 1 dozen shucked oysters at the same time kidneys are added. One cup sliced, sautéed mushrooms may also be added along with a splash of Madeira to the meat filling just before turning into crust.

LANCASHIRE HOT POT

Traditionally prepared from mutton, this hearty country English meat pie is yet another version of steak and kidney pie and shepherd's pie.

3 to 4 lamb kidneys
2 pounds boneless lamb stew meat, trimmed of excess fat
2 pounds potatoes, peeled and sliced
3 onions, thinly sliced
3 carrots, sliced
salt and freshly ground pepper to taste
12 oysters (optional)
1 tablespoon cornstarch
2 cups beef stock
4 tablespoons butter, melted

Wash and clean kidneys according to Steps I and II in basic instructions; cut in half lengthwise. Place layers of lamb, potatoes, onions, carrots and kidneys in a casserole, seasoning each layer with salt and pepper and ending with potatoes on top. If oysters are used, layer along with other ingredients. Combine cornstarch with cold stock; pour over all. Drizzle with melted butter. Cover tightly with lid and cook in a 275° oven for 2-1/2 to 3 hours.
Serves 6 to 8

PORK CISTE

3 pork kidneys
vinegar
6 thick center-cut pork chops
1/2 pound pork liver, chopped
2 medium onions, sliced
1 large carrot, sliced
1 tablespoon chopped parsley
1/2 teaspoon thyme
1 bay leaf
salt and freshly ground pepper
2 cups beef stock
1 recipe ciste (following)

Soak and clean kidneys according to Steps I and II in basic instructions, using vinegar in soaking liquid; drain and slice into bite-size pieces. Place chops vertically around inside edge of medium saucepan. Fill center of pan with kidneys, liver, onions, carrot and seasonings. Pour in stock just to cover the vegetables. Cover and simmer gently for 30 minutes.

In the meantime, prepare ciste. Roll out to fit diameter of saucepan. Lay pastry over vegetables, allowing rib bones to pierce pastry. Press to fit snuggly against the vegetables. Pan should be deep enough to allow for at least an inch of rising. Cover and cook gently over low heat for 1 hour. Serve in the saucepan. Loosen edges with sharp knife and cut into 6 wedges.
Serves 6
Note: This dish may also be cooked, uncovered, in a 375° oven for 1 hour, or until crust is golden.

Variation: Follow the above recipe, substituting all lamb meats for the pork. As per basic instructions, lamb kidneys need not be soaked.

CISTE

2 cups flour
1 cup minced kidney suet
1/2 cup milk
1 teaspoon baking powder
1/2 teaspoon salt

Combine flour, suet, baking powder and salt in a bowl. Cut with pastry blender until mixture resembles small peas. Add milk and stir until ingredients are well blended. Roll out on a pastry board to desired size. Use for topping meat pies.

TRIPE, ETC.

Although the definition of tripe is often confined to stomachs of ruminants only (even-toed, hoofed animals with a three- or four-chambered stomach such as the cow, sheep, deer, etc.), here tripe refers to the edible stomach of any butchered animal. Tripe has long been a mainstay of man's diet but it has been a food representing extremes. In Paleolithic times, before the advent of pottery and bronze, the stomach paunch of a hog served as the first cooking vessel. Stuffed with the hunter's kill, it was waterproof and heatproof enough to be hung over an open fire. The nomadic Scythians, likewise, followed this procedure. The herdsmen stripped the flesh from an animal, packed it into the stomach bag and then cooked the entire thing over a fire made from the dried bones of the animal. (Some stomachs had a capacity of 30 to 40 gallons, depending on the animal—sheep, goats, horses or cattle.) Fellow nomads of the Scythians in the Gobi desert prepared braised camel's paunch or roasted camel's hump—slaughtering their beasts of burden only after they were too old to perform.

A pig's paunch, served in vinegar and silphium (an herb that has since become extinct), was a delicacy of ancient Greece. In fact, Callimedon, a notorious contemporary gourmand, was ridiculed about his intense love for tripe. It was said that while most men would be willing to die for their country, Callimedon undoubtedly would give up his life for a boiled paunch. And rennet, a derivative of the stomach lining, was used by the Greeks, as well as by the Romans, Arabs and others, for curdling cheese, a practice which remains today.

Tripe rose in popularity in the classic Italian kitchen in the late 1300's and has been popular ever since. In 15th century Italy a potage made of tripe was served, and *busecca,* a rich thick tripe soup from Lombardy has become one of the best-known tripe dishes of today.

Beatie was a popular preparation of tripe in Northern Europe in the 18th century. A concoction made with blood, a good quantity of fat, some flesh, lungs and heart, it was packed into a stomach paunch and suspended over the fire to cook. The Scots have their version of this dish called haggis, made with either deer or, today more commonly, sheep. The animal's liver is mixed with other ingredients and stuffed into the stomach paunch to cook. It is traditionally served to the music of kilted bagpipers with some neat whiskey (het pint), clapshot (a dish of turnips, potatoes and chives) and black bun (fruit cake).

During the 18th century in America, pepper pot soup, most often identified with the Pennsylvania Dutch, was created by the head chef of the Revolutionary Army forces to save George Washington's troops from starvation at Valley Forge. With the gift of several hundred pounds of tripe from a nearby butcher and peppercorns donated by a Germantown patriot, the hearty "belly-comforting" pepper pot was invented, sharing the glory of a victory over the Red Coats.

Tripe is also part of the Eskimo diet. They regard the partially digested contents of the stomach as a special treat, possibly because of the flavor resulting from the fermentation.

Intestines, the long series of tubes connecting the stomach with other organs, have likewise been savored by many throughout history. During the 15th century in the market stalls of the Aztec capital of Tenochtitlan, cooked foods, giblets and "tripas" were sold, "tripas" being synonymous with the guts or entrails of the wild deer, the most commonly butchered animal of the day. These stalls may be regarded as the forerunner of the current French and British triperie, a specialty shop where tripe and other offal may be purchased, including intestines, calf's and sheep's heads, brains, sweetbreads, udders, feet, tongue, heart, liver, spleen and kidneys.

In the United States, the slaves on the plantations in the South were given leftovers from the hill which included chitterlings (small pork intestines). Chitterlings, or chitlins, soon became one of the most revered Southern dishes. Intestines, specifically the margut (intestines of an unweaned calf), were essential to the son-of-a-bitch stew of the cowboys of the Western plains. Although what went into the stew depended on the trail chef, the addition of margut and the cooking of it over a fire of buffalo chips made it authentic.

Today, intestines are eaten in a variety of ways in many cultures—the stuffed and spit-roasted kid or lamb intestines of Greece and Italy; *cordula,* seasoned grilled lamb intestines of Sardinia; and, of course, their use as casings for all kinds of sausages. One of the most succulent preparations for intestines is done in Hawaii. A pig is starved for two weeks, then fed only rice for one week. The pig is killed and roasted, never having been dressed. The intestines, stuffed with rice, are eaten along with the flesh and innards of the animal.

PREPARATION OF TRIPE

Tripe in its broadest sense may refer to the edible stomach of all butchered animals. More specifically it has been used to refer only to the stomach of ruminants, even-toed, hoofed animals that have a 3- or 4-chambered stomach, including the cow, sheep, etc. In this book we use the term tripe in recipes only when referring to the stomach of a cow, which is sold in pieces rather than whole. There are generally 2 types of beef tripe available from your butcher. That which comes from the walls of the paunch or rumen (the large first compartment of the stomach of a ruminant) is called plain or flat tripe. It has a slippery texture. The other kind of tripe, which comes from the walls of the reticulum (the second stomach of a ruminant), is referred to as honeycomb tripe, named so because of its honeycomb-like appearance.

All tripe from the butcher is very white. This is a result of the lengthy and tedious processing (soaking in lime, then in brine and boiling, much the same as the cure for olives) that is completed before its arrival on the wholesale-retail market. Be aware that the subsequent cooking times vary considerably, depending on the extent of this processing.

Flat and honeycomb tripe are interchangeable in the recipes that follow, unless otherwise noted. Honeycomb tripe is usually more tender than the flat variety, and requires at least 30 minutes less cooking time. Adjust cooking times in recipes accordingly. Although the stomach of a sheep or pig may be referred to as tripe in the broad sense of its being stomach, because it is most often sold whole for stuffing, we have referred to it as stomach rather than tripe. These animal stomachs have the slippery texture of flat or plain tripe.

Step I: Cleaning and Parboiling
Wash tripe well, rub with salt and rinse thoroughly. Then, if called for in recipe, parboil tripe in salted water (1 tablespoon salt per 1 quart of water) for 15 minutes. Drain, discarding water. Proceed with recipe.

A pig's or sheep's stomach is generally cleaned the same way as tripe. However, remaining membranes and excess fat should be removed from the lining. Turn the stomach inside out for stuffing. Parboiling of a stomach may or may not be necessary, depending on the particular recipe.

Step II: Court Bouillon
Place tripe in court bouillon to cover and simmer, covered, for 1 to 3 hours, or until tender, depending on size of pieces and extent of precooking. Reserve stock for soup base and stews if not to be used in the recipe. Proceed with recipe.

Ingredients for court bouillon:
1 onion, stuck with 2 cloves
2 stalks celery with tops
3 to 4 sprigs parsley
1 carrot
1 bay leaf
8 peppercorns
1 teaspoon thyme (optional)
water to cover

BROILED TRIPE

Following Steps I and II in basic instructions, clean, parboil and cook tripe until tender, about 1-1/2 hours. Drain. Cut into bite-size pieces. Dip into flour, then into melted butter and finally into fine French bread crumbs. Broil, smooth side up, for 3 to 4 minutes; turn and continue broiling until nicely browned. Serve with tartare sauce or lemon wedges.

FRIED TRIPE

The preparation is simple. Following Steps I and II in basic instructions, clean, parboil and cook tripe until tender, about 1-1/2 hours. Drain and cut into strips. Roll in fine French bread crumbs and drop into hot oil. Or if you prefer, the pieces may be dipped in beaten egg, then rolled in bread crumbs and fried. It's important to maintain the oil temperature, so don't fry too many pieces at once.

Variation: Rather than deep-frying tripe, sauté tenderly cooked strips of tripe in melted butter, after dusting individual pieces with flour. Sauté equal proportions of sliced green peppers and sliced onions in a separate pan. Combine tripe with onions and green peppers in a dish and pour a Béchamel sauce over all (see Basics).

69

PEPPER POT SOUP

3 pounds honeycomb tripe
1 veal knuckle
2 onions, chopped
1 bay leaf
1 stalk celery, including top
2 leeks, including tops, cut in half
2 sprigs parsley
1 sprig thyme
1 tablespoon salt
1 teaspoon freshly ground black pepper
dash of cayenne
1 or more dried red chilis, finely
    chopped
4 potatoes, peeled and diced
1 bell pepper, seeded and diced
2 tablespoons chopped parsley
1/3 cup flour
1 cup evaporated milk
1/3 cup butter

Clean and parboil tripe according to Step I in basic instructions; cut into 1/2-inch dice. Place veal knuckle, onions, bay leaf, celery, leeks, parsley, thyme and 4 quarts water into a large stock pot. Bring to a boil and skim any scum that rises to the top. Simmer, covered, 2 hours.

Strain broth; then remove meat from knuckle bone and dice. Return meat to pot along with tripe, salt, pepper, cayenne and chilis and simmer, covered, 1-1/2 hours longer. Add potatoes, bell pepper and parsley; cook another 20 minutes. Blend flour and milk together; gradually add to the soup mixture until slightly thickened. Add butter. Serve very hot in large bowls with plenty of crusty bread.
Serves 8 to 10

TRIPE & POTATO SOUP

2 pounds tripe
1/4 pound bacon or salt pork,
    well rinsed and diced
2 stalks celery, including tops,
    chopped
2 onions, chopped
1 carrot, scraped and diced
1 bay leaf
salt and freshly ground pepper to taste
1 small cabbage, shredded (about
    2 cups)
4 potatoes, peeled and diced
    (about 2 cups)
2 leeks, chopped

Clean and parboil tripe according to Step I in basic instructions. Rinse in cold water; drain. Cut into 1/2-inch dice. Sauté bacon in a skillet to render fat. Add celery, onions and carrot; cook for 5 minutes. Place bacon mixture in a stock pot with the tripe, bay leaf and a little salt and pepper. Cover with 3 quarts water and simmer 1 hour. Add cabbage, potatoes and leeks to the stock and adjust seasonings. Simmer, covered, 1 hour longer. Serve very hot.
Serves 6

BEAN CURD SOUP WITH PIG'S STOMACH AND TAILS

1 pig's stomach
2 pigs' tails, cleaned and cut in
    1-1/2-inch pieces
8 black forest mushrooms, soaked to
    soften and sliced
1 1-inch piece choong toy*
    (preserved turnip)
10 jujube dates* (Chinese red dates)
1 teaspoon salt
1/4 pound bean curd stick*, soaked
    to soften and cut in 2-inch
    lengths, or
1 pound tofu* (fresh bean curd
    cake), cut in 1-inch squares

Clean pigs' tails according to Step I in basic instructions of preparation of tails. Prepare pig's stomach according to Step I in basic instructions, parboiling tails at same time; drain, discarding water. Return both meats to pot and cover with 2-1/2 quarts fresh cold water. Add mushrooms, preserved turnip, jujube dates and salt and bring to a boil. Reduce heat, cover and simmer for 2 hours until stomach is tender.

Remove stomach, add bean curd stick and continue cooking for 30 minutes; if tofu is used, cook only 15 minutes. Slice stomach into 1/2x2-inch pieces; return to pot. Heat through and serve. The pigs' tails and stomach are delicious as a side meat dish, dipped in soy or oyster sauce.
Serves 6 to 8
*Available in Oriental markets

MENUDO

The Mexicans are convinced menudo is one of the best panaceas for a hangover. Though we cannot attest to this fact, we feel it is one of the greatest pots of soup (which can likewise be made into a stew). By tradition, an authentic menudo is cooked over a hickory or mesquite fire.

2 calf's feet, or
1 veal knuckle
4 pounds tripe
4 cups nixtamal hominy*, rinsed, or
2 28-ounce cans hominy, drained
2 onions, chopped
4 cloves garlic, finely chopped
1 tablespoon crushed oregano
2 tablespoons chopped fresh coriander
salt and freshly ground pepper to taste

Wash calf's feet and simmer in 6 quarts water in a covered stock pot for 1 hour. (This step may be eliminated if veal knuckle is used, as it goes in with the tripe.) Wash tripe and cut into 1x2-inch pieces, or smaller. Add tripe to calf's feet along with hominy, onions, garlic, oregano, coriander, salt and pepper. (Canned hominy is added the last hour of cooking.) Bring to a boil, cover, reduce heat and simmer for 3 to 4 hours. Serve, providing dishes of chopped onions, chopped fresh coriander and chili peppers for each person to add to his liking.
Serves 10 to 12
*White fermented corn available in Mexican markets. Though canned hominy may be substituted for nixtamal, the resultant taste does not compare. If you really want to make an authentic menudo, it's worth the effort of hunting down this ingredient.

TRIPE, ETC.

GOLDEN TRIPE

2-1/2 pounds tripe
approximately 3 cups court bouillon
1 clove garlic, finely chopped
1/2 cup finely chopped parsley
1/4 cup olive oil
1/4 pound bacon, finely chopped
1 onion, thinly sliced
salt and freshly ground pepper to taste
4 eggs
5 tablespoons freshly grated
    Parmesan cheese

Wash tripe; cook in court bouillon according to Step II in basic instructions, about 1-1/2 hours. Drain, reserve stock and cut into 1-1/2-inch squares. Sauté garlic and parsley in 2 tablespoons olive oil until garlic is golden. Remove with slotted spoon. Add the remaining oil, bacon and onion slices and sauté until onions are limp. Add garlic mixture, tripe, salt and pepper. Simmer 2 to 3 minutes. Add 1/2 cup reserved stock; cover and cook over low heat about 30 minutes. Just before serving, beat eggs together with Parmesan cheese. Pour this mixture over tripe; stir lightly and cook just until eggs are set, about 1 or 2 minutes. Mixture should have a creamy consistency. Serve immediately.
Serves 6

CURRIED TRIPE STEW

2 pounds tripe
3 tablespoons peanut oil
2 cloves garlic, finely chopped
1 slice fresh ginger root,
    finely chopped
1 onion, sliced
1 8-ounce can tomato sauce
1 cup chicken or beef stock
1 to 2 tablespoons curry powder
1 teaspoon salt
1/2 teaspoon white pepper
4 carrots, peeled and cut in chunks
1 bell pepper, cut in chunks
fresh coriander for garnish

Clean and parboil tripe according to Step I in basic instructions. Drain; cut into 1-inch dice. Heat oil in pan; add garlic, ginger and onion and sauté. Add tripe and a little more oil if necessary; sauté until lightly browned. Then add tomato sauce, stock, curry powder, salt and pepper. Bring to a boil, cover and simmer 1 hour. Add carrots and continue to cook 25 minutes. Add bell pepper and cook 10 minutes longer. Garnish with coriander. Serve with steamed rice.
Serves 4 to 6

TRIPE GRATINÉE

2-1/2 pounds tripe
1/4 cup diced bacon
1 onion, sliced
1 sprig rosemary
2-1/2 cups beef stock
1 cup sliced mushrooms
4 tablespoons butter
6 toasted French bread rounds,
    dried out in the oven
freshly grated Parmesan cheese

Wash, clean and parboil tripe according to Step I in basic instructions. Drain; cut in thin strips. Sauté bacon in large frying pan to render fat. Add onion and cook until lightly browned. Add tripe and rosemary and cook for 5 minutes. Add stock and simmer slowly for 1-1/2 hours or more, until tripe is very tender, adding more stock if necessary. Sauté mushrooms in butter 3 minutes. Add to the tripe the last 15 minutes of cooking time.
In the meantime, prepare bread rounds. Place each slice in individual ovenproof serving dishes. Add tripe with its broth and sprinkle with Parmesan cheese. Place under broiler a few minutes until golden; serve immediately with crisp green salad.
Serves 6

TRIPE WITH SAUSAGE

2 to 3 calf's feet, split
1/2 pound chorizo sausage
3 pounds tripe
1 small unpeeled garlic bulb*
2 small bay leaves
3 sprigs parsley
2 cups chopped onion
1/4 pound Virginia ham, cut into
  1/2-inch dice
1 onion, chopped
2 cloves garlic, chopped
2 tablespoons olive oil
1-1/2 cups peeled, seeded and
  chopped tomatoes
1 or more dried red chilis,
  finely chopped
1 teaspoon paprika
salt and freshly ground pepper to taste

Clean and parboil calf's feet according to Steps I and II of basic instructions for preparation of feet. Clean and parboil tripe following instructions in Step I of tripe preparation. Cut tripe in 1-1/2-inch squares. Prick chorizos several times with a fork and braise in a little water for 5 minutes. Drain and set aside.

Tie garlic bulb, bay leaves and parsley loosely in a cheesecloth bag. Place in a large flameproof casserole along with the tripe, calf's feet, 2 cups chopped onion and 3 quarts water. Bring to a boil, cover and simmer 2 hours. Add ham and simmer another hour.

In the meantime, sauté the chopped onion and garlic cloves in olive oil until onion is transparent. Add tomatoes, chilis and paprika; reduce over high heat until liquid has almost entirely evaporated. Combine this mixture with some of the stock from the casserole and then pour mixture slowly back into the casserole, stirring constantly. Slice chorizos and add to pot; continue to cook, partially covered, for another 15 minutes. Remove the cheesecloth bag. Adjust seasoning with salt and pepper. Serve piping hot with lots of crusty sweet French bread.

Serves 6 to 8

*This means a whole head, not a single clove. This contributes a subtle aroma to the pot.

73

TRIPE WITH HARICOT BEANS

3 pounds tripe
4 tablespoons butter
4 tablespoons diced salt pork,
    well rinsed
6 small onions, finely chopped
1 stalk celery, chopped
2 carrots, chopped
1 sprig sage
1 14-ounce can Italian plum tomatoes,
    chopped
salt and freshly ground pepper
1 cup beef stock
3 cups cooked haricot (white) beans
freshly grated Parmesan cheese

Wash, clean and parboil tripe according to Step I in basic instructions; drain and cut into narrow strips. Continue with Step II; drain. Heat butter and salt pork over medium heat. Sauté onions, celery, carrots and sage until golden brown. Add tomatoes and cook for 10 minutes. Then add tripe, salt, pepper and stock. Bring to a boil, reduce heat and cook 30 minutes. Add beans and adjust seasonings. Continue cooking 10 minutes longer. Serve with Parmesan cheese.
Serves 6

TRIPE ESPANOLE

3 pounds tripe
1 onion, chopped
1/4 cup olive oil
2 cloves garlic, mashed
1 16-ounce can stewed tomatoes, or
2 cups peeled and chopped tomatoes
1 bay leaf
salt and freshly ground pepper to taste
1 teaspoon crushed oregano
1 dried red chili, seeds removed
    and finely chopped
1 4-ounce jar pimientos, cut in pieces

Wash tripe and cut into long strips. Cook according to Step II in basic instructions, about 45 minutes; drain. In the meantime, make tomato sauce. Sauté onion in olive oil until transparent. Add garlic, tomatoes, bay leaf and remaining seasonings; simmer, covered, for 15 minutes. Remove bay leaf. Add tripe to sauce and cook until tender, about 1 hour. Add pimientos just before serving.
Serves 8

Variation: Prepare Tripe Espanole as directed. Spoon onto slices of toasted, buttered bread. Then sprinkle with grated hard Monterey Jack and Parmesan cheese. Garnish with sliced ripe olives and place under broiler until golden. Makes a rich winter luncheon entrée.

TRIPE À LA MODE DE CAEN

This is one of the world's classic recipes and probably can be singled out as the most famous of all innard recipes. It requires long, long, slow cooking. Short cuts definitely cannot produce the same results. In France, history records that this dish was baked in communal ovens. Today it may be purchased at the charcuterie.

5 pounds honeycomb tripe, cut
   in 1-1/2-inch squares
2 calf's feet
1/4 pound salt pork, rinsed and sliced
2 cloves garlic, finely chopped
4 onions, sliced
3 leeks, sliced
5 carrots, sliced
4 stalks celery, sliced
salt and freshly ground pepper to taste
bouquet garni (see Basics)
1-1/2 cups dry white wine
1 cup Calvados or applejack
beef stock
chopped parsley for garnish

Prepare tripe according to Step I in basic instructions, cutting after parboiling. Prepare calf's feet according to Step I for preparation of feet; split and chop into 3-inch lengths. Line a large earthenware casserole with the salt pork. Then arrange alternate layers of the vegetables and tripe. Salt and pepper each layer and place bouquet garni about in the middle of the casserole. Place the calf's feet on top. Add wine, Calvados and stock to fill the casserole. Cover with a tight-fitting lid. Cook in a 250° oven for 8 to 10 hours, or overnight. Remove the bouquet garni and serve bubbling hot with French bread. Serves 8 to 12

TRIPE MARMITE

This dish is much like tripe à la mode de Caen, but requires less cooking.

2-1/2 pounds honeycomb tripe
2-1/2 pounds pigs' feet, cleaned
2 leeks, chopped
2 carrots, chopped
2 stalks celery, chopped
2 onions, sliced
2 sprigs parsley, chopped
2 cloves garlic, finely chopped
salt and freshly ground pepper to taste
1/4 teaspoon freshly ground nutmeg
1/8 teaspoon ground cloves
1/2 teaspoon thyme
1-1/2 cups beef stock
1-1/2 cups dry white wine
2 tablespoons butter
1/2 pound mushrooms, sliced

Prepare tripe according to Step I in basic instructions; cut into 1-1/2-inch squares. Prepare pigs' feet according to Step I in preparation of feet. Split and chop into 3-inch lengths. Combine vegetables. Mix salt, pepper, nutmeg, cloves and thyme together. Put a layer of tripe and pigs' feet into a large flameproof casserole; top with a layer of vegetables and sprinkle with seasonings. Repeat until all ingredients are used. Pour stock and wine over all, adding more in equal amounts if necessary to cover. Bring to a boil, reduce heat, cover and simmer over very low heat for 4 hours.
Heat butter in saucepan and sauté mushrooms for 2 to 3 minutes; add to casserole last 15 minutes of cooking time. Skim off any fat and serve very hot with French bread and wine.
Serves 8

TRIPE VINAIGRETTE

Following Steps I and II in basic instructions, clean, parboil and cook tripe until tender, about 1-1/2 hours. Drain. Cut into strips and cover with vinaigrette dressing (see Basics). Chill well. Good served as an hors d'oeuvre or first course.

Variation: Substitute sauce Gribiche (see Basics) for the vinaigrette dressing.

HAGGIS

To many a Scotsman, haggis conjures up fond memories, this being the national, historical dish of his home- land. If you've not heard of it before, haggis simply is a pudding made from a sheep's heart, lungs and liver, com- bined with finely chopped suet, oat- meal and onions, then stuffed into a sheep's paunch and boiled. (Some pur- ists challenge the inclusion of liver; in the following recipe the lung has been omitted because it is illegal to sell it in the United States.) Though passion- ately acclaimed a Scottish dish, the origin of haggis dates back to the days of Homer. Nevertheless, it has been immortalized by Robert Burns in his lines To a Haggis (1786) and savored by his countrymen on many a Bobbie Burns' night.

1 sheep's stomach
1 sheep heart
1 sheep liver
1/2 pound fresh suet (kidney leaf
   fat preferred)
3/4 cup oatmeal
3 onions, finely chopped
1 teaspoon salt
1/2 teaspoon freshly ground pepper
1/4 teaspoon cayenne
1/2 teaspoon nutmeg
3/4 cup stock

Wash and parboil stomach according to Step I in basic instructions. Put in cold salted water for several hours. Cover heart and liver with cold water, bring to a boil, reduce heat, cover and simmer for 30 minutes. Chop heart and coarsely grate liver. Toast oatmeal in a skillet on top of the stove, stirring frequently, until golden. Combine all ingredients and mix well. Loosely pack mixture into stomach, about two- thirds full. Remember, oatmeal ex- pands in cooking.

Press any air out of stomach and truss securely. Put into boiling water to cover. Simmer for 3 hours, uncovered, adding more water as needed to main- tain water level. Prick stomach several times with sharp needle when it begins to swell; this keeps the bag from burst- ing. Place on a hot platter, removing trussing strings. Serve with a spoon. Ceremoniously served with "neeps and nips"—mashed turnips, nips of whiskey and mashed potatoes.

PIG'S STOMACH BRAISED IN SOY SAUCE

1 pig's stomach
3/4 cup soy sauce
1/4 cup sugar
1/4 cup sherry
1/2 teaspoon 5-spice powder
1 whole star anise
2 slices fresh ginger root
1 piece dried tangerine peel
2 green onions with tops, cut up
2 sprigs coriander (optional)

Prepare pig's stomach according to Step I in basic instructions, parboiling for 10 minutes. Discard water. Bring 2 cups water to a boil with remaining ingredients; add pig's stomach, reduce heat, cover and simmer for 1-1/2 hours until stomach is tender. Turn stomach over every half hour to insure even flavoring and coloring. When tender, lift out stomach and cut in 1/2x1-1/2-inch strips; reserve juices for other uses. Garnish with some extra green onion and coriander, if desired. Serve hot or at room temperature. Serves 6

Note: The reserved juices should be strained, put into a glass jar and stored in the refrigerator. Use for flavoring meats or vegetables in stir-frying or reuse in braising or marinating other meats such as pigs' feet, tails or ears, tongue, chicken and duck feet.

STUFFED PIG'S STOMACH, CHINESE STYLE

1 pig's stomach
2 slices fresh ginger root
2 cups cooked rice (sweet rice preferred)
1 cup chopped water chestnuts
6 black forest mushrooms, soaked to soften and diced
1/2 cup smoked ham (Virginia ham preferred), diced
1 piece dried tangerine peel, soaked and finely chopped
3 tablespoons peanut oil
1/2 cup chicken stock
2 tablespoons soy sauce
2 tablespoons dry sherry
1/2 cup chopped green onions and tops
1 teaspoon fried sesame oil*
peanut oil for deep-frying
soy sauce
dry mustard

Following instructions in Step I, wash and clean pig's stomach, removing membranes and excess fat from lining. Cook in salted water with ginger slices for 1-1/2 hours, or until tender. Drain and pat dry with paper towels. (Reserve stock for later use, such as bean curd and pigs' tail soup.) Cook rice and keep hot.

Sauté water chestnuts, mushrooms, ham and tangerine peel in the oil for 2 minutes. Add stock, soy and sherry; cover and simmer for 10 minutes. Add green onions and sesame oil, then combine with hot cooked rice in a large bowl. Toss well.

Fill the pig's stomach and truss, catching edges securely. Place oil in wok or deep cooking vessel and heat until very hot. Deep-fry stomach until crisp and golden on both sides. Drain; let rest 5 minutes. Slice and serve with soy sauce and hot mustard (made by mixing dry mustard with a little hot water to desired consistency).
Serves 6 to 8
*This is the dark seasoning oil available at Oriental markets.

STUFFED SOW'S MAW

Whenever there was a sow to be slaughtered, there was a sow's maw to be stuffed, according to the Pennsylvania Dutch. You may not be willing to take it from the beginning, but your butcher may rescue one for you.

1 pig's stomach
1 pound ground pork
1 pound pork sausage
4 raw potatoes, peeled and
    finely diced
1 onion, chopped
2 stalks celery, chopped
1/4 teaspoon marjoram
1/4 teaspoon ground sage
1/2 teaspoon pepper
1 cup apple cider
1 cup beef stock

Following directions in Step I, wash and clean pig's stomach, removing membranes and any excess fat from lining; pat dry with paper towels. Combine all other ingredients except liquid and pack loosely in stomach; truss or secure with skewers. Place on a rack in a shallow roasting pan; pour cider and stock over, cover with foil and roast in a 325° oven for 3 hours. Uncover last half hour, basting skin until it is crisp and golden brown. Remove trussing string or skewers; cut in thick slices with a very sharp knife. Serves 6 to 8

PREPARATION OF INTESTINES

Intestines are used in braising, stewing and frying (as in chitterlings) almost as much as they are used for casings. The way you plan to serve them, of course, will determine the variety and size. Pork, lamb and beef intestines, all, are eaten. However, pork intestines are more commonly used for casings. Generally speaking, there are 3 categories of pork intestines. The small, sheer pork intestines are called *menus,* or *menuises,* and are used to encase small sausages such as link sausages or Italian dry salami. The caecum, called the *sac* or *poche* in French, is slightly larger and expands to about 1-1/2 to 2 inches when stuffed and cooked or dried, as in the French *andouilles.* The colon, or *chaudin,* is the largest intestine and is used in the making of *andouilles* and other sausages.

Intestines for both casings and cooking unstuffed may be purchased fresh or partially cooked. Casings that are purchased partially cooked are also preserved in a brine or are salted down. (The salted version resembles the drop line of fishing tackle.) They must be soaked to soften and to remove saltiness. Although this book uses only innards in the forcemeats, forcemeats made of any ingredients may be prepared and loosely stuffed into any variety of intestine to make sausage.

Step I: Cleaning

To clean intestines, first cut them into manageable lengths, about 1 to 2 feet. Then run cold water through the opening, using a funnel or faucet nozzle, until water runs clear. Remove any excess fat.

If intestines are to be used other than for sausage-making, they may be slit lengthwise and cleaned. Partially cooked chitterlings, or chitlins, are often found on the butcher's counter already slit. Although we suggest that you clean the intestines before using, many ethnic cultures prefer them to be left alone. The undigested food within the intestines is regarded as a delicacy, much like the tomalley of the lobster and crab "butter."

Step II: Soaking

Soak intestines at least 1 hour in a bath of 1 tablespoon salt or baking soda to 1 quart water. Rinse well again and proceed with recipe.

Cooking Time

Pork and beef intestines require 2 to 4 hours of simmering; veal and lamb intestines are more tender and therefore require only 2 hours of simmering at the most. If intestines are used for casing in sausage-making, cooking time is further reduced because the skin is stretched considerably in stuffing. (See boudin, page 87, for directions on preparing and cooking sausages.)

CHITLINS

Hog's jowls, collard greens and chitter-lings or chitlins (the small intestines of a hog) are probably the most famous of all soul food.

5 pounds chitterlings
3 cloves garlic
1 lemon, halved
1 teaspoon freshly ground pepper
2 whole cloves
1 teaspoon thyme
2 sprigs parsley
2 bay leaves
2 onions, quartered
1 teaspoon salt
1/4 teaspoon mace
1/4 teaspoon allspice
1 tablespoon marjoram
1/4 cup cider vinegar
1 cup tomato sauce
cayenne to taste

If chitterlings are purchased pre-cooked, prepare according to Step II in basic instructions; if they are purchased fresh, prepare according to Steps I and II. Place chitterlings in a large pot with water just to cover; add all ingredients except tomato sauce and cayenne. Simmer, covered, for 3 to 4 hours, or until tender. (Timing will vary depending whether fresh intestines or partially cooked chitterlings are used.) During the last 30 minutes of cooking, add tomato sauce and cayenne. Serve with coleslaw and corn bread.
Serves 8 to 10

Variation: Follow the preceding recipe, omitting cloves, mace, allspice, marjoram, vinegar, tomato sauce and cayenne. Add 2 stalks celery and 2 or more dried red chilis, crushed, to cooking liquid. After chitterlings are tender, drain well, pat dry and cut into 2-inch squares. Dip in beaten egg and roll in cornmeal, and fry in hot deep fat. Drain on paper towels. Serve with Tabasco sauce.

BULGARIAN BAKED LAMB INTESTINES

2 pounds lamb intestines
3 carrots, scraped and sliced
1 stalk celery, sliced
3 sprigs parsley
2 tablespoons butter or vegetable oil
8 green onions, whites only, chopped
3 cloves garlic, finely chopped
2 to 3 tomatoes, seeded and chopped
3 eggs
1 tablespoon flour
1 cup yoghurt
freshly grated Parmesan cheese

Prepare intestines according to Steps I and II in basic instructions. Put in a pot with carrots, celery, parsley and 2 cups water. Bring to a boil, reduce heat, cover and simmer 45 minutes. Strain vegetables, reserving stock. Cut intestines into 1-inch pieces and set them aside.
Heat butter in skillet and sauté onions and garlic until transparent; add tomatoes and cook 3 to 4 minutes longer. Place mixture in a 1-1/2-quart baking dish; add intestines and 1/2 cup reserved stock. Bake at 350° for 20 minutes. Beat eggs, flour and yoghurt together and pour over intestines; Sprinkle with Parmesan. Return to 400° oven and bake until firm and golden, about 10 minutes.
Serves 6

BURRITOS DE TRIPAS

An American cook might put ground beef, possibly boiled beef, into burritos, but the Mexicans use pork and tripas more commonly in theirs. (Tripas in Spanish refers to any section of the digestive tract, from the plain tripe to the actual intestines, which are often braided together in long strands before cooking.) In San Francisco there are restaurants that specialize in burritos filled with these meats. First the meats are cooked in huge pots of simmering lard that has been seasoned with a salt-water brine until very tender. (Water allows lard to boil; salt will not dissolve in lard.) Then they are chopped and placed into the tortillas. Cooking the meat this way not only retains the juices, but makes them very tender and flavorful, but not the least bit greasy.

lard
tripe or intestines (usually pork)
steamed flour or corn tortillas
hot refried beans (see Basics)
Mexican rice (see Basics)
tomato salsa (see Basics)

Clean tripe according to Step I in basic instructions. If using intestines, prepare according to Step I in basic instructions for intestines. In a large pot, melt enough lard to cover tripe. Add at least 1 cup of water in which some salt has been dissolved. Bring to rolling boil, being careful hot fat does not splatter on you. Add tripe and simmer over low heat, uncovered, for 2 to 3 hours until tender. Meat will not be crisp. Drain well and blot with paper towels; chop meat. Place meat, refried beans and rice along with salsa to taste in center of warm tortilla; roll up.

Variation: Tongue may be cooked and used in this manner also.

TRIPAS DE LECHE

Mexicans regard this dish as one of the greatest of all delicacies. The *tripas de leche,* known also as the milk intestines or marrow gut, refers to the tubular canal connecting the stomachs of an unweaned calf. Needless to say, they are very tender and require little cooking.

The intestines are washed, cut into 2-inch lengths and then slowly deep-fried in lard until crisp. They may also be roasted or grilled; however basting is essential to avoid drying out. By tradition, they are eaten with tortillas and tomato salsa (see Basics).

CHARCUTERIE

Though *charcuterie* in French literally means a shop where one buys cooked meats prepared in a wide variety of ways, pork in particular, we feel the definition of the art of charcuterie should include any forcemeat stuffed into any intestine or stomach. By using this broader definition, charcuterie may be said to have commenced with the first man of Paleolithic times stuffing a filling into a stomach paunch and cooking it. Men of all cultures have been preserving meats, making forcemeats and "stuffing" ever since.

A banquet dish of India in the first millenium B.C., called *mandaliya,* was actually a sausage made from entrails stuffed with spices and marrow and roasted over an open fire. Then in medieval times, cooked foods such as forcemeat and baked meats made their first appearances in marketplaces. These items were in the form of sausages as well as terrines. Today, the French have their *andouille* and *boudin* (coinciding with the hog slaughter); the Germans have their *weisswurst* and *bockwurst;* the Turks and Greeks have their *kukerets* or *kokoretsi,* made of lamb intestines that have been wrapped around finely minced heart, kidney, liver and sweetbreads and seasoned with oregano, dill, lemon juice and olive oil; the Poles have their *kielbassa;* the Italians have their *mortadella;* and the Mexicans have their *chorizo.* The Israelis have a different method of preparing sausages; they make use of poultry necks—of turkey, chicken, goose or duck.

The recipes within this chapter are limited to forcemeats or stuffings requiring variety meats. We hope you will use your imagination to create others.

CHARCUTERIE SPICE

Every merchant in France has his special blend of quatre-épices (four spices). Likewise, we've blended our own. However, we've expanded it to include five spices.

4 tablespoons freshly ground white
    pepper
1 tablespoon freshly grated nutmeg
1 tablespoon ground ginger
1/2 teaspoon cinnamon
1/2 teaspoon ground cloves

Combine all ingredients and store in a jar with a tight-fitting lid.

FROMAGE DE TÊTE VINAIGRETTE

1 beef head or 2 calves' heads
pickling brine (see Basics)
1 bay leaf
6 whole cloves
6 peppercorns
1/2 teaspoon powdered sage
1/4 to 1/2 cup wine vinegar
1/2 cup thinly sliced pimiento-
    stuffed olives
1/2 teaspoon freshly ground pepper
vinaigrette dressing (see Basics)

Remove eyes, brains, ears, snout and most of fat from head. Soak in several changes of cold water to remove blood. Place in pottery or glass crock, cover with salt brine and store in a cool, dark place for 7 to 10 days. Cover with cold water and parboil for 15 minutes; discard water. Return to pot with fresh cold water, bring to a boil and add bay leaf, cloves, peppercorns, sage and vinegar. Reduce heat, cover and simmer for 3 to 4 hours until meat comes away from bones.
Remove head from pot and remove and chop all meat from bones. Strain and reduce stock to 4 cups. Cool and chill until partially set. Then stir in pepper, olives and chopped meat. Pour into an oblong mold. When set, cut in strips or slices. Serve with vinaigrette. Garnish with chopped parsley, chives or green onions.
Serves 10 or more

CHOPPED CALF LIVER

1 1-pound piece calf liver
4 tablespoons butter
1 cup finely chopped onions
1/2 cup chopped parsley
1 teaspoon salt
1/2 teaspoon freshly ground pepper
1/4 teaspoon freshly grated nutmeg

Bake liver in a 325° oven for 30 minutes. Cool, remove membranes and veins; chop finely. Heat 2 tablespoons butter and sauté onions and parsley until onions are transparent. Mix with liver and chill briefly. Blend with remaining butter. Season with salt, pepper and nutmeg. Pack into crock or mound on lettuce leaves. Serve with thin slices of rye bread.

Variation: Follow the above recipe, adding 1/4 teaspoon tarragon, fresh lemon juice to taste and 1 chopped hard-cooked egg.

POTTED PORK LIVER PÂTÉ

1 pork liver, membranes removed
1 pound lean pork
1 pound pork fat
salt and freshly ground pepper
1 clove garlic, finely chopped
2 tablespoons finely chopped shallots
1/4 teaspoon charcuterie spice
    (page 83)
1 pound pig's caul*
strips of pork rind as needed
1 cup dry white wine
1/2 cup Cognac
4 to 5 marrow bones, cut in
    1-inch pieces
1 cup sliced carrots
1 onion, sliced
1 bouquet garni (see Basics)

Grind together coarsely the meats and fat. Season with salt and pepper to taste. Add garlic, shallots and charcuterie spice and mix well. Spread a piece of pig's caul flat on the table. Put the ground meat mixture in the center. Wrap the caul around it and bring the ends together, forming into a large mound.
Line a Dutch oven or earthenware casserole with pork rind. Place mound in casserole and drizzle with wine and Cognac. Surround with marrow bones and vegetables; submerge bouquet on the side. Bake, uncovered, in a 250° oven for 2-1/2 hours, basting fre-

quently with cooking liquid. When the mound is well glazed and meat is done, remove and cool. Chill. Serve at room temperature.
Note: If pâté is not to be eaten within a week, remove to clean earthenware casserole or terrine and cover with melted pork fat to 1 inch above pâté. Tie a piece of waxed paper or foil over the top; cover. May be stored up to a month in the refrigerator.
*Pig's caul is the fatty membrane investing the intestines.

PAUL'S PÂTÉ

2 pounds chicken livers
4 tablespoons vegetable oil
1 large dill pickle, cut in chunks
1/2 onion, cut in chunks
1/2 bell pepper, cut in chunks
2 hard-cooked eggs, finely chopped
1 teaspoon prepared mustard
1 teaspoon paprika
1/2 teaspoon freshly ground pepper
1 or more teaspoons salt
2 tablespoons mayonnaise

Sauté livers in oil until firm; drain on paper towels. Then grind livers, using a medium blade, with pickle, onion and bell pepper. Mix well with remaining ingredients. Pack in pottery crocks.

QUICK LIVER PÂTÉ

1/2 pound liverwurst, at room
    temperature
6 tablespoons sweet butter,
    at room temperature
1 tablespoon grated onion
1 tablespoon chopped chives
2 tablespoons finely chopped parsley
2 tablespoons Cognac
salt and freshly ground pepper

Cream together liverwurst and sweet butter. Add remaining ingredients and form into a smooth mound or pack into crocks.

CHICKEN LIVER TERRINE

1/2 pound chicken livers
4 tablespoons butter
1 onion, cut in chunks
2 cloves garlic, finely chopped
1 pound ground pork
2 eggs, beaten
1/2 teaspoon charcuterie spice
  (page 83)
1/2 teaspoon rosemary or thyme
2 teaspoons salt
1/2 teaspoon freshly ground pepper
1/4 cup Cognac
1/2 cup pistachio or pine nuts
3 tablespoons flour
blanched bacon slices or salt pork
  strips as needed
1 bay leaf

Sauté livers in butter until firm. Set aside and let cool. Then grind, using a fine blade, with onion and garlic. Combine with remaining ingredients. Line terrine with overlapping bacon slices and press mixture into mold. Top with bacon slices and place bay leaf in center. Cover with a tight-fitting lid and bake in a 350° oven for 1 to 1-1/2 hours, or until liquid in pan and fat run clear. Cool 15 minutes, then weight down and cool thoroughly. Store in refrigerator, but serve at room temperature.

COUNTRY TERRINE

2 cups diced smoked tongue
1/4 cup Cognac
1 pound side pork, diced
1 pound ground pork
1 pound pork liver
2 pounds ground veal
1 teaspoon each marjoram and basil
2 tablespoons chopped parsley
1 clove garlic, finely chopped
1 teaspoon charcuterie spice (page 83)
1 teaspoon each salt and freshly
  ground pepper
blanched bacon slices as needed
1 bay leaf

Have butcher grind together ground pork, liver and ground veal. Marinate tongue in Cognac for 30 minutes. Mix together all ingredients until well blended. Line a large earthenware baking dish or terrine with overlapping bacon slices. Mound mixture in mold and top with bacon slices; place a bay leaf in center. Bake in a 350° oven for 1-1/2 to 2 hours, or until fat runs clear. Cool and chill. Serve at room temperature.

ANDOUILLE

The charcuteries of France are filled with andouilles and andouillettes (the smaller variety)–a dry pork sausage commonly made from pork tripe, even heart and spleen, and put in a pig-intestine casing. Butchers, in fact, are acclaimed for their individual recipes. Andouilles, made from large pig intestines, are most often eaten cold as hors d'oeuvre (cut in thin slices as salami), whereas the andouillettes made from small intestines are usually served hot, accompanied by sautéed or mashed potatoes or braised sauerkraut.

The sausages are first poached in lightly salted water and allowed to cool. They are then lightly slashed, brushed with butter and grilled. The most famous of these sausages come from Brittany, Vire, Nancy, Strasbourg, Caen and Lyons, to mention only a few. Our recipe is similar to the sausages from Nancy because the spleen and heart are included in the forcemeat.

5 pounds pork trimmings from
   neck, including blood
1 pork heart
1 pork spleen
1-1/2 tablespoons salt
1 tablespoon freshly ground pepper
1 teaspoon charcuterie spice
   (page 83)
1 onion, finely chopped
4 cloves garlic, finely chopped
1/2 cup chopped parsley
large pork intestines
sea salt

Grind meats, using a medium blade. Add remaining seasonings and mix well. Put in a crock and store in a cool place overnight. Stir well the next day and stuff the intestine three-quarters full; tie off in 12-inch lengths. Roll in sea salt and let stand in salt 8 to 10 days. Remove from salt and hang to dry for 2 months. To serve, simmer in lightly salted water for about 1-1/2 hours (see procedure for boudin, page 87). Serve warm or chilled.
Makes 8 to 10 pounds sausage

Variations: This same mixture may be stuffed in small pork intestines to made andouillettes; reduce the cooking time. Or stuff the mixture in a double-thickness of pig's caul (see instructions for potted pork liver pâté, page 84); do not salt or hang to dry.

BLACK PUDDING
(Sausage)

1 pork heart
1 pound pork spleen
2 pounds pork kidneys
1/2 pound pork fat, sow's belly or fat back
2 to 3 pounds pork trimmings from butt or neck, including blood
1/2 cup dry sherry
2 teaspoons crushed oregano
1 teaspoon caraway seeds
1/2 teaspoon dill
1 tablespoon salt
1-1/2 teaspoons freshly cracked pepper
1 pound pork intestines for casings

Clean and prepare pork intestines (see Steps I and II, intestines, page 79); soak in water until ready to use. Prepare heart and kidneys according to basic instructions (see pages 37 and 55, respectively). Remove membranes from spleen.

Grind meats, including fat and trimmings, using a medium blade. Then combine with remaining ingredients and mix well. Fill the intestines three-quarters full, using a sausage stuffer to simplify the procedure. Tie off in desired lengths. Hang sausages in well-ventilated, cool room for 2 to 4 hours to blend flavors. Place in refrigerator overnight.

Cook either by boiling (see instructions for boudin, following) or broiling. Cooking time varies, depending on thickness of sausage. Serve with sautéed apple rings, braised sauerkraut and boiled potatoes. Or serve on pumpernickel bread with hot mustard and thinly sliced onion rings.

BOUDIN
(Blood Sausage)

1/2 pound pork fat, cut in 1/4-inch dice
2 cups minced onions
1 cup rich beef stock
2 tablespoons lard
2 tablespoons flour
2 cups evaporated milk or fresh half-and-half
1 quart fresh pork blood, strained through a fine sieve
1 teaspoon charcuterie spice (page 83)
1 tablespoon finely minced parsley
1/2 cup finely minced mushrooms, sautéed in
1 tablespoon butter
pork casings (page 79), cut in 18-inch lengths

Combine pork fat, onions and stock in large saucepan. Bring to a boil, reduce heat, cover and simmer 1 hour. Blend lard and flour in another saucepan; gradually add milk, stirring constantly.

Continue cooking until sauce begins to thicken. Stir in onion mixture. Bring to a boil and simmer 10 minutes, stirring constantly. Remove from heat and pour all at once into pork blood. Add charcuterie spice, parsley and cooled mushrooms.

Have ready 18-inch lengths of cleaned casings, tied at one end with white string. Fill casings three-fourths full with blood mixture, using a funnel (3/4 inch in diameter) to facilitate filling. Tie open end with string. To cook, drop prepared sausages, a few at a time, into boiling salted water; simmer gently for 25 minutes, uncovered. Prick any sausages that rise to the surface with a pin to allow air to escape, thus preventing sausages from bursting. Remove sausages with a slotted spoon and let cool. Refrigerate. (Sausage may be stored up to 3 days in the refrigerator, or frozen.)

To serve, make diagonal slashes in the skin of the sausage and grill over hot charcoal. Or, sauté, unslashed, in a little butter and oil. Serve with sautéed apple slices or on a bed of braised sauerkraut.

GALANTINE OF CHICKEN

1 4-1/2-pound roasting chicken,
    boned, with wings and legs
    attached
2 teaspoons salt
2 tablespoons butter
1 onion, chopped
1 pound ground veal
1/2 pound chicken livers, diced
1 slice bread, soaked in
2 tablespoons milk
2 hard-cooked eggs, finely chopped
2 eggs
1/4 cup Port or Madeira
2 tablespoons chopped chervil
1/4 cup heavy cream
1 teaspoon paprika
salt and freshly ground pepper
1 cup dry white wine
2 cloves garlic
1 carrot, sliced
3 sprigs parsley
lemon slices, parsley and radishes
    for garnish

This is where a friendly butcher is worth a million dollars if you've never boned a chicken or turkey before. Chop extracted meat and rub inside skin well with salt. Heat butter and sauté onion until transparent. Add veal and livers. Combine this mixture with chicken, bread, eggs, Port, chervil, cream, paprika, salt and pepper.

Lay chicken skin open flat on a table. Heap forcemeat in center and truss with white string. (This procedure is more easily handled if another person holds raw skin together while you are sewing.) Brush well with melted butter. Tie securely in muslin or cheesecloth, tying in several places to hold the shape. Place in a large pot with wine, garlic, carrot, parsley sprigs and 2 cups water. Simmer gently for 1 hour or until tender, turning once. Remove from heat and let cool in stock. Carefully remove to platter and chill overnight. To serve, garnish with lemon slices, parsley and radishes. Remove wings and legs and then cut into crosswise slices.

Serves 8 to 10

Variation: When galantine is chilled, decorate with triangles of hard-cooked egg white, pimiento strips and string beans. Make an aspic by dissolving 1 tablespoon unflavored gelatin in 2 cups clarified chicken stock; heat stock and then add juice of 1 lemon in which 1/2 teaspoon tarragon leaves have been soaked and strained out. Set pan of hot stock in a bowl of ice until the aspic becomes syrupy. Brush the partially set aspic over the galantine and chill. Pour leftover aspic on a platter or cookie sheet, 1/4 inch thick. Chill until set; chop and surround galantine with chopped aspic.

(Galantine de Poulet).

STUFFED PIG'S FEET

The French, Italians and Chinese stuff the entire foreleg of the pig. Since pigs in the United States are not slaughtered in the same manner as in these countries, we have used just the pig's foot, which is more commonly available. Depending on seasoning, this dish is known as jambe de porc farcie or zampino on the European continent, and is highly regarded.

2 pig's feet, skin intact
court bouillon to cover (page 93)
1/2 pound brains (any kind), cleaned
   and parboiled 10 minutes (page 7)
1/4 cup chopped parsley
1/4 cup Cognac
2 tablespoons soft bread crumbs
1/2 teaspoon charcuterie spice
   (page 83)
3 tablespoons pistachios
3 tablespoons chopped mushrooms
2 tablespoons chopped shallots
1 egg
1 teaspoon salt
1/2 teaspoon freshly ground pepper

Choose large meaty pig's feet with skin intact. Slit underside of pig's feet just to the toes. Carefully remove meat and bones, leaving toes undisturbed and skin intact. Soak the skins in cold water to cover and 1 tablespoon salt for 1 hour, or until ready to use. Boil meat and bones in court bouillon to cover for 1-1/2 hours until tender; remove from pot. When cool enough to handle, remove all meat and gelatinous parts; mince and combine with remaining ingredients.

Pat the skins dry; sew cut edges together with white string, forming a tube. Stuff with prepared forcemeat and mold into original shape. Wrap each foot separately in several layers of cheesecloth, covering the opening well to prevent mixture from bursting out. Wrap several times again and tie in several places to hold shape. Place in a large pot so feet lay flat on the bottom. Cover with boiling water, return to the boil and simmer for 1-1/2 hours. Do not unwrap. Cool, then chill. Unwrap just before slicing. A spectacular culinary coup de maître.

Variation: Follow the preceding recipe, substituting 3/4 pound ground pork and pork casings for pig's feet. Fill in casings (see page 79) and cook in simmering water for 35 minutes (see instructions for cooking boudin).

HEADS, FEET & TAILS

The head of an animal has had culinary stature since man first began his search for food. The head has been honored with pageantry by nobility, yet eaten by peasants in grateful acceptance of God's gift of nourishment. Heads have been roasted over open fires, boiled for rich, gelatinous stocks and cleaned of their flesh for headcheese ("potted heads" in England) or forcemeats.

It is an ancient custom in China for the fish head to be served to the oldest (and most honored) member of the family; the cheeks and soft pockets behind the eyeballs are regarded as the greatest delicacy of all. This custom was carried over to 19th century France, when the carp's head was served to the most distinguished guest at the table, although the French considered the tongue of the carp to be the juiciest morsel of all.

In medieval England, the boar's head was the gala dish of every banquet. The arrival of the head (previously roasted and decorated) was heralded by trumpeteers, with ladies and gentlemen of the court parading joyously behind. This tradition became associated with Christmas and there's even an old English Christmas carol written in praise of the boar's head. The ceremony is still celebrated at Queen's College in Oxford and has even spread to California: At the Awahanee Hotel's Christmas dinner in Yosemite National Park, a boar's head is symbolically presented before the table.

A 15th century Italian cookbook gives a recipe for veal's head dipped in garlic juice, and states that all heads of four-footed beasts are heavy foods, but nourishing, and work wonders for increasing male fertility. Alexis Soyer, the great English chef and author of *A Shilling for the People,* created several very delicious recipes for sheep's heads. Pigs' cheeks also were prized in England. They were first smoked, then boiled in seasoned water and served cold.

In France during the early 1800's, one of the most fashionable dishes of the day was calf's head served in its hide. The eyes were thought to be the most tantalizing, then jowls, temples, ears and tongue; each of these was served with a small portion of the brain. Curiously enough, there was such an overabundance of sheep's heads in Argentina in the late 1800's that they were actually used to fill quagmires so roads could be built (land fill in modern-day terminology).

A present-day delicacy in Turkey is known as *bash*. A sheep's head is roasted until crisp, then brought to the table and ceremoniously cracked open before all who are present. The brain is brought out first, then the tongue, followed by the other meats. It is a culinary ritual.

Tails, snouts, ears and feet have all shared a bit of culinary eminence, too. The Sumerian tribes (2400 to 2300 B.C.) developed a breed of sheep called fat-tailed sheep, noted for an especially fat tail which represented about one-sixth of the sheep's total body weight. A single tail might weigh as much as 10 pounds and was a rich source of high-quality fat—unquestionably the delicacy of the time. The sheep's tail achieved even greater fame in the pastoral society of Baghdad; *alya*, fat rendered from the sheep's tail, was the basis of practically every dish.

The nose or snout of an animal made its first debut in the kitchen when a dog was used in Babylonian times to unearth a kind of truffle from the ground. In later times, in France, the pig replaced the dog in this important task. Led on truffle-hunting expeditions, the pig gained stature in man's mind because he could find food as well as be used for food. De la Reynière mourned over the dishonor paid the pig, saying: "Everything in a pig is good. What ingratitude has permitted his name to become a term of opprobrium?"

The Puerto Rican fishermen also had an affectionate attitude toward a pig's nose. Pigs were always carried in a ship's hold when the sail plan took them out of sight of land. When it came time to return to port, the pig was brought on deck and used as a compass, for he instinctively pointed his snout toward land. The Romans' affection, however, was exhibited in a different manner. The pig to them was a culinary masterpiece. They ate the paunch, testicles, matrix, cheeks, ears, snout, feet, entrails and cracklings, as well as the fat. This culinary appreciation of the pig persisted throughout history—especially in China, England, France and even America. Many Americans are familiar with Pennsylvania Dutch scrapple or ponhause—a mixture of cornmeal, pork trimmings and spices. Benjamin Franklin is also known to have waxed enthusiastic for pigs.

Trotters or feet have been an important part of many cuisines. When cooked, they produce gelatin, a nutritious substance high in protein that solidifies when it cools. Pigs' trotters were a favorite of the ancient Greeks and Romans. The Chinese ate them along with all appendages, accurately believing they strengthened the body. In fact, postpartum mothers are still served pickled pigs' feet for this very reason.

Consommé has been made from calf or poultry feet since the 15th century in Italy. One recipe called for pheasant, partridge or pigeon feet combined with cinnamon, sage and other spices. The Italians thought consommé healthy for old and hearty alike. And, of course, it was indispensable to *haute cuisine,* when there was a *à la gelée* of everything.

Pieds de Porc St.-Menehould is probably the most famous of all French preparations of feet. It is said that this dish was indirectly responsible for Louis XVI's death. It was during a fateful stop to fill his belly with pigs' feet in the village of St.-Menehould that he was recognized by Jean-Baptiste Drouet, a member of the Convention, and apprehended, later to be beheaded.

In America, "pocket soup" or "portable soup" was one of the main foods of explorers and travelers. A forerunner to the bouillon cube, it was actually concentrated stock made from veal trimmings and pigs' trotters. Nowadays, pigs' feet are generally available in most markets; however, sheep's trotters are more difficult to find. Unfortunately, in the United States, sheep's trotters are commonly rendered into fertilizer, used for tallow material or sent to the glue factory rather than sold on the retail market for food.

PREPARATION OF HEADS, FEET, TAILS, EARS AND SNOUTS

The edible foot of any animal is often called a trotter. However, for the sake of clarity, we will call them feet, with one exception: Through common usage, sheep's trotters have become the accepted term for the feet of both lamb and sheep.

Step I: Cleaning
Remove any hairs on heads, feet, tails, ears or snouts by singeing over an open flame or plucking. Scrub well (using a vegetable brush if desired) and then sprinkle with salt, rubbing it into the skin. Rinse well with cool water; pat dry. Remove any excess fat. Poultry feet (chicken, duck or turkey) must be stripped of their outer scaly skin; plunge them in boiling water 1 minute, as you would do before peeling tomatoes. Proceed with recipe.

Step II: Parboiling
Parboil in salted water (1 teaspoon salt for each quart water) for 5 minutes. Drain, discarding water. This step serves the purpose of ridding the meat of running blood as well as clinging meat, fat or bone residue, thereby adding clarity to sauces.

Step III: Court Bouillon
Cook in following court bouillon. Bring meat to boil in court bouillon, reduce heat, cover and simmer for 1-1/2 to 3 hours, depending on type and size of meat. Follow recipe instructions for cooking times.

Ingredients for court bouillon:
2 stalks celery, with tops
1 onion, stuck with 2 cloves
1 carrot
8 peppercorns
bouquet garni (see Basics)
6 allspice berries (optional)
1/2 lemon (optional)

If the court bouillon is not used as part of the recipe, it may be strained and reserved for a rich soup stock or added to stews and sauces. Note: We prefer adding the lemon to a court bouillon when cooking pigs' feet, snouts, ears or tails as it enhances the flavor and helps cut the richness created by their gelatinous quality.

HEADS

CALF'S HEAD SOUP

1 calf's head
1 onion, peeled and halved
1 bunch parsley
1 teaspoon crushed marjoram
1 bay leaf
2 tablespoons salt
1 teaspoon grated lemon rind
1/2 cup chopped parsley
1 egg
5 tablespoons flour
salt and freshly ground pepper to taste
1/4 cup vegetable oil
3 tablespoons butter
1/4 cup dry sherry or Madeira

Wash calf's head well; parboil for 5 minutes in water; drain, discarding water. Return to pot with 3 quarts fresh cold water; bring to a boil and simmer for 3 hours, skimming from time to time to remove scum. Then add onion, parsley, marjoram, bay leaf and salt and continue cooking another hour. Strain stock; set aside. Remove all meat from bones.

Make forcemeat by grinding the meat, lemon rind and chopped parsley together. Add egg, 2 tablespoons flour, salt and pepper; shape into small balls the size of a walnut. Fry in oil until golden.

Melt butter and add remaining 3 tablespoons flour in pot; cook 3 or 4 minutes to brown slightly. Add reserved stock, cooking to thicken slightly. Add sherry just before serving. Return meatballs to pot.

Serves 8

LAMB'S HEAD SALAD

1 lamb's head, whole
1 onion, chopped
1 carrot, peeled and chopped
1/2 celeriac, peeled and chopped
1 bay leaf
1 teaspoon salt
freshly ground pepper to taste
2 tablespoons olive oil
1 tablespoon white wine vinegar
1 tablespoon chopped parsley
1 tablespoon chopped fresh dill
1 teaspoon chopped fresh celery leaves

Cover lamb's head with water and parboil for 10 minutes; discard water. Return to pot with fresh water to cover, adding vegetables, bay leaf, salt and pepper. Bring to a boil, reduce heat, cover and simmer for 1 hour, or until meat falls completely away from bones. Strain cooking liquid and reserve for later use. Cut meat into bite-size pieces, chill and before serving mix with oil, vinegar, parsley, dill and celery leaves.

Serves 6 to 8

Variation: Substitute the head of a pig or calf for lamb's head.

LAMB'S HEAD SOUP

For a rich soup, thicken the reserved broth from the preceding recipe with 3 tablespoons cream and 1 egg yolk. Combine cream and egg yolk in a bowl and gradually add a cup of the hot stock. Stir this mixture into remaining stock and heat through.

CRISP ROASTED PIG'S HEAD

1 pig's head, cleaned and
    tongue removed
1 teaspoon 5-spice powder
2 tablespoons salt
1/2 cup mien see* (ground
    brown bean sauce), or
1/2 cup oyster sauce*
1/4 cup bourbon
1 cup honey, combined with
1 cup boiling water
watercress or coriander
    sprigs for garnish

Prepare pig's head according to Step I in basic instructions. Place head in a colander in the sink and pour a kettleful of boiling water over. Let cool. Combine the 5-spice powder, salt, bean sauce and bourbon. Slash meat on underside of head and rub half of the spice mixture into the meat. Rub the remaining spice mixture onto the skin. Place head upright on a rack in a large baking pan. Bake at 375° for 1-1/2 hours. Lower heat to 325° and continue cooking for an additional 2 hours, or until the meat is cooked through, basting the skin well every 30 minutes with the honey-water mixture. (Cooking time will depend on the size of the head.) If ears begin to brown too quickly during cooking period, wrap them with foil. When head is done, remove to platter and garnish with watercress or coriander. Chop head into pieces and serve with sweet vegetable relish (see Basics) or plum sauce.

*Available in Oriental markets

95

SHEEP'S HEAD

Sheep's heads traditionally have been served (and relished) by the peoples of sheep-herding countries–from England and Scotland to the Middle East. Unfortunately, as the pastoral life gives way to modern technology, these native dishes are rapidly disappearing. It isn't often that you come across a freshly killed lamb, but if you're out in the country, you might find a rancher who is willing to save the head for you after the slaughter.

1 sheep's head
rose water
2 to 3 onions, sliced
salt and freshly ground pepper

Remove snout altogether as it is very difficult to clean. With a sharp knife clean head, scraping carefully; also singe off any hairs. Place head in a pot with water to cover and simmer 30 minutes, skimming away any scum that rises to the surface. Drain; pat dry. Rub with rose water and return to pot. Smother with onions, season with salt and pepper and add fresh water just to cover. Bring to a boil, reduce heat, cover and simmer head for about 3 hours. Serve hot or cold with vinaigrette dressing (see Basics).

ROASTED LAMB'S HEAD

1 lamb's head, skinned and cleaned
1/3 cup olive oil
1/4 cup dry red wine
1-1/2 teaspoons crushed oregano
2 cloves garlic, finely chopped
1/2 teaspoon salt
1/2 teaspoon freshly ground pepper

Remove eyes and tongue of lamb's head. Then parboil head in water to cover for 10 minutes. Simmer tongue for 30 minutes in salted water; skin. Return to lamb's mouth.
Make a marinade by combining remaining ingredients; pour over head while warm and marinate for 1 hour, turning occasionally. Bake in a 325° oven for 1-1/2 hours, basting from time to time. Place on a bed of parsley, surrounded by cherry tomatoes. Decorate with a garland of daisies. To serve, crack head down center and remove meat.

SCRAPPLE

A Pennsylvania Dutch-inspired break-
fast dish.

4 pounds pork scraps with bones, or
1 hog's head, split
1 teaspoon salt
6 peppercorns
3 whole cloves
1 bay leaf
2 cups cornmeal
1 onion, finely chopped
1/4 teaspoon cayenne
1/2 teaspoon freshly ground nutmeg
1/2 teaspoon or more ground sage
salt and freshly ground pepper

Parboil pork scraps or head, in water
to cover, for 10 minutes. Drain; discard water. Return to pot with fresh
water to cover, salt, peppercorns,
cloves and bay leaf. Bring to a boil,
cover and simmer for 3 hours, or until
meat falls off the bones easily. Strain
stock; reserve. Remove all meat from
bones and chop; set aside.
Reheat stock; gradually add cornmeal,
stirring constantly until thick, about
15 minutes. Add meat, onion, cayenne, nutmeg and sage; adjust seasonings with salt and pepper. Pour into 2
greased loaf pans. Refrigerate until set.
Slice and fry for breakfast. Will keep
in the refrigerator up to 1 week.
Serves 12

THE FAT PIG CASSEROLE

2 pig's ears
2 pig's feet
1 pound pork butt, cut in 1-inch cubes
1/4 pound salt pork or bacon ends,
    well rinsed
3 tablespoons vegetable oil
2 tablespoons butter
1 onion, thinly sliced
1/2 cup dry white wine
2 stalks celery, finely chopped
2 carrots, finely chopped
1 head cabbage, quartered
3/4 pound sliced cotechino or
    Italian sausage

Prepare pig's ears and feet according to
Step I in basic instructions. Cut ears in
half and chop pig's feet roughly with a
cleaver; cut salt pork into 1/4-inch
slices. Put all meat, except pork butt,
into pot with water to cover and simmer 1 hour. Remove meat with slotted
spoon; cut ears into thin strips; remove
any loose bones.
Heat oil and butter in large skillet and
sauté onion until lightly browned. Add
pork cubes and brown on all sides.
Add wine, celery, carrots, pig's ears
and feet, salt pork and 2 cups stock.
Simmer for 30 minutes. Place cabbage
wedges on top of meat and continue
cooking 30 minutes longer. Finally
add sausage, cover and cook 20 minutes. Skim off any excessive fat.
Serves 8

PICKLED PIGS' EARS, CHINESE STYLE

2 pounds pigs' ears
4 whole star anise
3 slices fresh ginger root
1/2 cup white vinegar
1/4 cup sugar
1 teaspoon salt

1 cup white vinegar
1 cup sugar
1 tablespoon thinly sliced fresh
   ginger root
3 cloves garlic, sliced
1 teaspoon salt
1 cup sliced carrots
1 cucumber, unpeeled, seeded and
   cut in chunks
1 red onion, cut in chunks
1 bell pepper, cut in chunks

MORAHAN'S VEGETABLE SLICER.

Prepare pigs' ears according to Steps I and II in basic instructions; drain. Return to pot with water to cover and first 5 ingredients listed above. Bring to a boil and simmer 1 hour; let meat cool in liquid. Discard liquid and cut ears into 1/2x1-inch slices.

In the meantime, bring 3 cups water to a boil with remaining vinegar, sugar, ginger, garlic, salt and carrots. Turn off heat when boiling point is reached. Cool mixture to room temperature.

Then add cucumber, onion, bell pepper and sliced pigs' ears. Chill in refrigerator for at least 4 hours to blend flavors. Will keep up to 1 week refrigerated. Serve as an appetizer or a cold meat side dish.
Makes 2 quarts

Variations: Pigs' snouts may be prepared in the same manner. Add 1 cup fresh sweet pineapple chunks at the same time as the vegetables.

PIGS' EARS SALAD

1 pound pigs' ears
3 whole star anise
1 2-inch slice fresh ginger root
1 cup raw carrots, cut in thin julienne
1 cucumber, peeled, seeded and cut
   in 2-inch julienne
2 green onions, tops only, slivered
   lengthwise and cut in 2-inch
   julienne
1/2 cup plum sauce or mango chutney,
   mashed
salt and freshly ground pepper
lemon juice to taste
butter lettuce leaves
toasted sesame seeds

It is important that all ingredients in this recipe be well chilled. Prepare pigs' ears according to Steps I and II in the basic instructions. Discard water and return ears to pot with water to cover, star anise and ginger. Bring to a boil, reduce heat, cover and simmer for 45 minutes, or until ears are tender. Remove ears, let cool and chill. Cut into very thin strips (1/8 inch).
Combine pigs' ears, carrots, cucumbers and onions and toss lightly with plum sauce. Season with salt and pepper and a little fresh lemon juice if a slightly tart flavor is desired. Serve on crisp lettuce and sprinkle with sesame seeds.
Serves 6

BOILED PIGS' FEET

This is a good procedure to follow if you want pigs' feet to remain whole. Wrapping them in cheesecloth not only helps keep their shape, but prevents the skin from breaking during cooking. It is important to keep the court bouillon at a low simmer. Choose smaller pigs' feet if gelatinous qualities are desired; larger feet offer more meat. After pigs' feet are cooked, they may be breaded, braised or served with any number of sauces, from mild to very piquant.

4 to 6 pigs' feet
court bouillon

Clean pigs' feet according to Step I in basic instructions. Wrap securely and tie in cheesecloth. Proceed with Step III, with the court bouillon. Simmer, covered, over low heat 3-1/2 to 4 hours, depending on size. Cool in stock. Remove cheesecloth. Place in dish and cover with stock, if not to be used immediately; otherwise, freeze. Proceed with following recipes.

BROILED PIGS' FEET ST. MENEHOULD

This is one of the great classic dishes of France. Traditionally the pigs' feet are wrapped in cheesecloth and simmered for 24 hours, then allowed to stand for another 24 hours until they become so tender that even the bones can be eaten. The following is a simplified version; the meat will be tender, but don't eat the bones!

pigs' feet, precooked in court bouillon
French bread crumbs

Prepare pigs' feet according to preceding recipe for boiled pigs' feet. Roll in bread crumbs and broil or grill until browned on all sides. Serve with a spicy sauce or Dijon-style mustard.

Variations: Follow above recipe, rubbing pigs' feet with olive oil or melted butter before rolling in bread crumbs. Good with tartare sauce, mustard sauce or Madeira sauce.
Follow above recipe, removing bones from pigs' feet before broiling. Dip in beaten eggs seasoned with dry mustard before rolling in bread crumbs. This is also good fried in butter.
Pigs' tails and ears may be prepared using any of the methods given above.

PICKLED PIGS' FEET

4 to 5 pounds pigs' feet
1 Bermuda onion, thinly sliced in rings
2 cups white vinegar
1 bay leaf
6 to 8 peppercorns
4 whole allspice
4 cloves garlic, halved
1 or more dried red chilis

Prepare and cook pigs' feet according to preceding recipe for boiled pigs' feet. Cool; unwrap and place in jars along with onion rings. Bring 2 cups water, vinegar, bay leaf, peppercorns, allspice, garlic and chili to a boil in a saucepan. Pour over pigs' feet and let cool. Place in refrigerator at least 24 hours before using to allow flavors to blend. They will keep up to 1 week, refrigerated.

Variation: Pigs' ears, snouts or tails may be substituted for the pigs' feet. Follow Steps I and II in basic instruction. These substitutions need not be wrapped in cheesecloth during cooking period.

CHICKEN FEET

Stock made entirely from chicken feet is very rich and gelatinous. The same holds true if chicken feet are added to a prepared chicken broth. Additionally, chicken feet added to any stew during the cooking period further enriches the sauce, thus enhancing the flavor. The best thing, however, is eating the chicken feet that are left. Dip them in a Tabasco-flavored soy sauce and eat as a meat side dish.

CHICKEN OR CALF'S FEET JELLY

2 pounds chicken feet, or
2 calf's feet, split
1 onion, quartered
2 carrots
1 stalk celery with leaves
1 clove garlic, crushed
1 teaspoon salt
4 peppercorns
2 bay leaves
2 hard-cooked eggs, sliced
1/3 cup lemon juice
1/2 cup pickles, chopped
lemons, quartered

Prepare feet according to Steps I and II in basic instructions. Place in pot with water to cover, onion, 1 carrot, celery, garlic, salt, peppercorns and bay leaves. Simmer at least 2 hours. Reduce stock to 1-1/2 quarts. Strain liquid into mold and set aside to cool. Slice thinly remaining carrot and blanch for 2 minutes. Add carrot along with remaining ingredients to jelled stock. Place in refrigerator until set. Slice for cold cuts or for a first course; garnish with lemon wedges. Cube to serve as an hors d'oeuvre; serve with prepared mustard.

Variation: Remove meat from feet, chop finely and add to jelly.

PIGS' FEET JELLY

A word on pigs' feet jelly. Any court bouillon, in which pigs' feet have been the only meat used, will make a marvelous jelly. (Of course, the same holds true for other feet, such as chicken or calves'.) This jelly is excellent served on salads or sliced into sandwiches or served on a cold buffet table.

Just strain the reserved stock through cheesecloth, add some vinegar or lemon juice to taste and pour into a loaf pan or mold. Chill in the refrigerator until set, about 4 hours. Other ingredients may be added if desired. One of our favorites is the addition of sliced rounds of hard-cooked egg, pimientos and olives to the partially set gelatin.

JELLIED PIGS' FEET & TONGUE

3 pig's feet
1-1/2 quarts or more court bouillon
1/2 pound smoked tongue, cooked
   and thinly sliced
1/3 cup dry white wine
1/3 cup white vinegar
1/3 cup sugar
1/2 teaspoon freshly ground pepper
1/8 teaspoon ground cloves
1-1/2 teaspoons salt
1/4 cup sliced pimientos (and
   diced, if desired)
watercress

Prepare pig's feet according to Steps I and II in basic instructions. Then cook in court bouillon to cover (1-1/2 quarts) according to Step III, about 3 hours or until meat is very tender. Remove feet, reserving stock. Let meat cool. Remove all meat from bones and dice; chill.

In the meantime, reduce stock to 3 cups. Add wine, vinegar, sugar, salt, pepper and cloves to stock. Bring to a boil and simmer for 5 minutes. Remove from heat, strain, let cool and chill until partially set. Remove from refrigerator; assemble.

To assemble, place a layer of the jelled stock in the bottom of a 1-1/2-quart mold. Layer a few slices of tongue on top, then another layer of gelatin with pimientos and diced pigs' feet (reserving some of the more gelatinous pieces for decorating sides and bottom of mold), repeating until all ingredients are used. End with a layer of tongue. Tuck the reserved meat into the sides of the mold. Smooth top with a thin layer of gelatin. Chill until set, at least 4 hours. Unmold and serve on a bed of watercress. Slice with a very sharp knife. Serve with Dijon or Pommerol mustard as a first course or on a cold buffet table.

SHEEP'S TROTTERS WITH LEMON SAUCE

12 sheep's trotters
1/2 cup lemon juice
2 tablespoons butter
1 teaspoon chopped fresh mint
2 egg yolks, beaten
salt and freshly ground pepper

Prepare feet according to Steps I and III in basic instructions, simmering in court bouillon. When done, remove all meat from bones and chop. Strain and reserve liquid. Heat 2 cups of the reserved stock in a saucepan with lemon juice, butter, mint and meat. Just before serving, combine about 1/2 cup of the heated stock with the egg yolks, stirring constantly; gradually add egg mixture back to the soup. Cook until smooth and thickened. Season with salt and pepper.
Serves 4 to 6

HOCHEPOT

2 pig's feet, split and cut in
    3-inch pieces
1/2 pound pigs' ears
2 pounds beef brisket
1-1/2 pounds veal shoulder
1 pound lamb shoulder
3 sprigs parsley
1 bay leaf
2 sprigs thyme
4 to 6 peppercorns
2 stalks celery, sliced
12 Polish sausages
3 carrots, peeled and cut in chunks
12 pearl onions or small boiling onions
2 leeks (tough stems removed), cut
    in chunks
1 head cabbage, quartered
salt and freshly ground pepper
butter

Prepare pig's feet and ears according to Step I in basic instructions. Put all meats, except sausages, in a pot and cover with water. Bring to a boil, skimming away any scum that rises to the surface. Repeat until all scum has disappeared. Then add herbs and celery, cover, and simmer for 2-1/2 hours. Add sausages, carrots, onions and leeks and continue cooking another 30 minutes. Add cabbage and cook, uncovered, 7 to 10 minutes longer, or until cabbage is tender. Remove meat and slice. Place in a warm casserole along with vegetables and a little of the stock. Serve with crusty bread.
Serves 10 to 12
Note: Reserve stock for a flavorful soup base. Meats in the recipe may vary depending on taste.

Variation: Follow the preceding recipe, substituting 3 coarsely chopped onions for pearl onions. Add 1 turnip and 2 potatoes, both peeled and cut in eighths, along with sausages and other vegetables. After vegetables are tender, remove with slotted spoon and mash to a purée, adding a little stock or heavy cream to make a smooth consistency. Season with salt and pepper. Mound in center of warm platter. Surround with sliced meats. Serve at once with a spicy mustard and pickles.

YUGOSLAVIAN SOUR SOUP

3 pounds pigs' feet, snouts or ears
2 carrots, diced
1 onion, diced
2 stalks celery, diced
1 parsley or celery root, peeled
    and diced
1 pound potatoes, peeled and diced
2 tablespoons butter or oil
2 tablespoons flour
1 clove garlic, finely chopped
juice of 1 lemon
salt and freshly ground pepper to taste

Prepare meat according to Step I in basic instructions. Quarter pigs' feet or cut ears and snouts into bite-size pieces. Cook meat in 2 quarts water along with carrots, onion, celery and root for 1-1/2 hours. If pigs' feet are used, remove from stock and remove all meat; dice and return to stock. Add potatoes and continue cooking 20 minutes longer.
In the meantime, make a roux by first heating oil in a small saucepan; add flour and garlic and cook until lightly browned. Thicken soup with this mixture. Add lemon juice just before serving and adjust seasonings. Serve this hearty soup with a basket of homemade bread.
Serves 4 to 6

WINTER MELON SOUP WITH DUCK FEET & GIZZARDS

2 pounds winter melon, pulp
  and seeds removed
1/2 pound duck feet (heads and wings
  may be substituted)
2 dried duck gizzards*, soaked to
  soften (fresh gizzards may be
  substituted)
6 to 8 black forest mushrooms,
  soaked to soften and quartered
  if large
6 to 8 jujube dates** (Chinese
  red dates)
1 piece dried tangerine peel,
  soaked until soft
1/2 cup Virginia ham or prosciutto,
  cut in small dice
salt to taste

Scrub skin of the winter melon, but do not remove. Cut in 1-1/2-inch cubes; set aside. Prepare duck feet according to Steps I and II in basic instructions, adding gizzards during Step II. Combine meat with winter melon, mushrooms, jujube dates and tangerine peel in 3 quarts water. Bring to a boil, reduce heat, cover and simmer for 1-1/2 hours until winter melon is soft and transparent. Add ham; adjust seasonings. Serve in soup bowls. Eat winter melon by scooping out flesh with a spoon and discarding skin. Eat the duck feet and gizzards, too.
Serves 6 to 8

*Dried duck gizzards have been salted in order to preserve them (this method has been used by the Chinese for hundreds of years). Before using in any recipe, soak the gizzards in hot water for 15 minutes. Their taste and texture resembles that of jerky. To prepare your own dried duck gizzards, salt fresh gizzards liberally. Hang to dry in a warm, breezy area until dried and hard. Store in a glass jar with a tight-fitting lid.

**Available in Oriental markets

SWEET & SOUR PIGS' FEET SOUP

The Chinese serve this rich, gelatinous soup to post-natal mothers to help them regain their strength. It's spicy, nutritious and warming.

4 pounds pigs' feet, split and halved
1 cup vinegar
1 cup brown sugar
3 tablespoons thinly sliced ginger root
2 teaspoons salt

Prepare pigs' feet according to Steps I and II in basic instructions; drain, discarding water. Return feet to the pot; add fresh water to cover, vinegar, sugar, ginger root and salt. Bring to a boil; reduce heat, cover and simmer 1-1/2 hours, or until pigs' feet are tender. Ladle into bowls and serve hot.
Serves 6 to 8

BRAISED PIGS' FEET

6 pigs' feet, split
3 onions, chopped
1 clove garlic, finely chopped
1 bell pepper, chopped
2 bay leaves
1/2 cup vinegar
2 dried red chilis, seeds removed
3 stalks celery, chopped
1 4-ounce can tomato paste
1 teaspoon paprika
salt and freshly ground pepper to taste

Prepare pigs' feet according to Step I in basic instructions. Cover with water and cook for 30 minutes; add remaining ingredients. Bring to a boil, reduce heat, cover and simmer for 1-1/2 hours. Serve very hot with rice.
Serves 6

PIGS' FEET AND TRIPE

5 pounds pigs' feet
2 pounds tripe (smooth tripe preferred)
4 strips bacon, cut in 1-inch pieces
2 cloves garlic, finely chopped
2 stalks celery, including leaves, sliced
1 bell pepper, diced
1/2 cup chopped parsley
1 to 2 dried red chilis, seeded and
  diced
2 teaspoons crushed oregano
2 teaspoons salt
1 teaspoon cracked black pepper
2 bay leaves
1 28-ounce can tomatoes, or
3 cups fresh peeled tomatoes
1/2 cup vinegar mixed with
2 cups water

Prepare pigs' feet according to Step I in basic instructions; split. Clean and parboil tripe according to Step I (see Tripe); cut into 1-inch squares.
Place pigs' feet in the bottom of a Dutch oven or flameproof casserole. Layer tripe, then bacon over them and sprinkle with chopped garlic. Mix celery and bell pepper with remaining herbs and spices and sprinkle over casserole. Tuck bay leaves into center and pour tomatoes, vinegar and water over all. Bring to a boil, reduce heat, cover and simmer for 2-1/2 hours or until meats are tender. Serve in bowls with French bread or over rice.
Serves 8 to 10

PIGS' FEET & SAUERKRAUT

6 pigs' feet, split
2 quarts sauerkraut, rinsed and drained
1 onion, sliced
1 apple, peeled and sliced
1 tablespoon caraway seeds
dry white wine
6 to 8 small potatoes, peeled

Prepare pigs' feet according to Step I in basic instructions. Place a third of the feet in the bottom of a heavy casserole or Dutch oven. Layer sauerkraut on top. Alternate remaining feet with a layer each of the onions and apples. Top with caraway seeds. Add wine to cover. Cover and simmer until the feet are tender, about 2 hours. Add potatoes and continue cooking 30 minutes longer.
Serves 6 to 8
Note: Frankfurters or pork sausages may also be added to the casserole, allowing just enough time for them to heat through.

TURKISH CALF'S FEET & WHITE BEANS

2 calf's feet, split and cut in
    3-inch lengths
4 tablespoons vegetable oil
2 onions, chopped
1-1/2 cups dried white beans (Navy
    or Great Northerns), soaked in
    water to cover overnight and
    drained
1/2 teaspoon ground ginger
1/2 teaspoon turmeric
1/4 teaspoon cayenne
6 eggs, shells uncracked (optional)*
salt and freshly ground pepper
1/4 cup chopped fresh coriander

Prepare feet according to Steps I and II in basic instructions. Heat oil in a flameproof casserole and sauté onions until golden brown. Add the feet and sauté until golden on all sides. Add the beans, ginger, turmeric, cayenne and uncracked eggs. Cover with cold water, bring to a boil, reduce heat, cover and simmer for 2-1/2 hours until meat falls away from bones. Season with salt, pepper and coriander. Serve hot with cucumber and yoghurt salad.
Serves 6
*The eggs are hard-cooked during the simmering of the stew. The whites take up the flavors of the stock and the yolks become very creamy.

CALVES' FEET, ITALIAN STYLE

6 calves' feet
2 tablespoons butter
4 tablespoons olive oil
1 onion, chopped
3 tablespoons tomato paste
1 tablespoon chopped fresh basil
3 tablespoons finely chopped parsley
1/4 teaspoon cinnamon
salt and freshly ground pepper to taste
freshly grated Parmesan cheese

Prepare feet according to Steps I and III in basic instructions, reserving stock. Remove meat from bones and cut into bite-size pieces. Heat butter and oil in a skillet and sauté onion until transparent. Add meat, 3/4 cup of reserved stock, tomato paste, basil, parsley and cinnamon and reduce to half over high heat. Season with salt and pepper. Sauce should be thick. Serve very hot with Parmesan cheese and pasta or polenta.
Serves 6

PIGS' FEET WITH BLACK BEAN SAUCE

2 pounds pigs' feet
2 tablespoons salted, fermented black beans (dow see)*, mashed
2 cloves garlic, finely chopped
1 slice fresh ginger root, finely chopped
1 piece tangerine peel, softened in warm water and finely chopped
3 tablespoons oil
2 tablespoons dry sherry
1 tablespoon soy sauce
1 cup chicken or pork stock

Clean pigs' feet according to Step I in basic instructions; split and cut in half again. Continue with Step II; drain. Make paste by mashing together black beans, garlic, ginger root and tangerine peel. Heat oil and immediately add black bean paste and pigs' feet, stirring and browning all the while. Add sherry, soy and stock; bring to a boil, cover and simmer 1 hour, or until feet are tender, but not falling apart. Check liquid from time to time, adding more if necessary to keep meat from burning. Serve with rice and stir-fried greens.
Serves 4

Variation: Chicken feet may be prepared using the same method.
*Available at Oriental groceries

PIGS' FEET, KOREAN STYLE

3 pounds pigs' feet
1 teaspoon salt
1 slice fresh ginger root
2 tablespoons peanut oil
2 tablespoons soy sauce
2 cloves garlic, finely chopped
1 tablespoon finely chopped fresh ginger root
1/2 teaspoon fried sesame oil*
1 tablespoon toasted sesame seeds, crushed
2 tablespoons chopped green onion
1 dried red chili, finely chopped, or 1/4 teaspoon cayenne

Prepare pigs' feet according to Steps I and II in basic instructions; drain split and quarter. (Reserve stock for other use.) Return feet to pot with fresh water to cover, salt and ginger root slice; bring to a boil, reduce heat, cover and simmer for 1-1/2 hours, or until tender. Remove pigs' feet and pat dry. Heat oil and stir-fry pigs' feet until golden brown. Then add soy, garlic, chopped ginger root, sesame oil, sesame seeds, green onion and chili. Cover, let steam rise to the top and serve with rice.
Serves 6
Note: Use reserved stock for a good soup, adding watercress and tofu; or Napa cabbage and green onions; or spinach and mushrooms.
*This is the dark seasoning oil available at Oriental markets.

PIGS' FEET WITH PLUM SAUCE

3 pounds pigs' feet, left whole
1/2 cup vinegar
1 teaspoon salt
2 tablespoons sugar
3 whole star anise
1 teaspoon fennel seeds
plum sauce
pickled ginger
green onions

Prepare pigs' feet according to Steps I and II in basic instructions; drain, discarding water. Return to pot with water just to cover, vinegar, salt, sugar, star anise and fennel seeds. Cover and simmer for 1-1/2 hours. (It is very important that the pigs' feet do not boil as it will break the skin and cause the meat to separate.) Remove feet from pot, drain and let cool. Then chill in refrigerator. When chilled, split in half lengthwise with a sharp cleaver and chop into 2-inch pieces.

Dip into plum sauce when eating and serve with pickled ginger and green onions. Serve as an entrée, first course or at a picnic.

Serves 4 to 6

BRAISED CHICKEN FEET WITH HOISIN SAUCE

2 pounds chicken feet
2 tablespoons hoisin sauce*
1 clove garlic, finely chopped
1 piece dried tangerine peel,
    soaked to soften and minced
1 teaspoon chopped fresh ginger root
1 tablespoon soy sauce
2 tablespoons dry sherry
1 teaspoon sugar
3 tablespoons peanut oil
1 tablespoon cornstarch, mixed with
1/4 cup water

Prepare chicken feet according to Step I in basic instructions. Combine hoisin, garlic, tangerine peel, ginger, soy, sherry and sugar in a bowl. Heat oil in a wok until hot and add chicken feet; stir well. Add the hoisin mixture, continuing to stir and browning lightly for 5 minutes. Add 1 cup of water, cover, reduce heat and simmer for 35 minutes. Bind juices with cornstarch mixture. Serve with rice and green stir-fried vegetables.
Serves 4 to 6
*Available at Oriental markets

CHINESE FRAGRANT BRAISED DUCK FEET

1-1/2 pounds duck feet
2 tablespoons soy sauce
2 tablespoons dry sherry
1 tablespoon sugar
1/2 teaspoon 5-spice powder
1 teaspoon finely chopped fresh
    ginger root
1 clove garlic, finely chopped
1 piece dried tangerine peel,
    soaked to soften and minced
3 tablespoons peanut oil
1 tablespoon cornstarch, mixed with
1/4 cup water
chopped fresh coriander and green
    onions for garnish

Prepare duck feet according to Step I in basic instructions. Combine soy, sherry, sugar, 5-spice powder, ginger, garlic and tangerine; marinate duck feet in this mixture at least 2 hours; drain, reserving marinade. Heat oil in wok and brown duck feet. Combine the marinade with 1 cup water; add to wok. Bring just to a boil, cover and simmer 1 hour. Bind juices with the cornstarch mixture. Garnish with coriander and green onions.
Serves 4 to 6

Variation: For fried and steamed duck feet, marinate duck feet as above. Drain feet well, reserving marinade. Fry duck feet in hot, deep oil until brown; drain. Then place in a shallow pyrex or ceramic baking dish. Drizzle 1 tablespoon of the reserved marinade over all and steam in large, covered pot or steamer above 2 inches of water for 40 minutes. Serve with rice and stir-fried greens.

TOSTADAS WITH PIGS' FEET & BEANS

2 cups heated refried beans
  (see Basics)
12 tortillas, fried crisp
1/2 cup grated dry Monterey Jack
  cheese
shredded lettuce
2 cups chopped meat from
  pickled pigs' feet (page 99)
2 avocados, sliced
6 to 8 radishes, sliced
1 onion, thinly sliced
tomato salsa (see Basics)

Spread beans over the tortillas. Sprinkle with cheese and shredded lettuce. Garnish with chopped meat, avocado slices, radishes and onion. Pour salsa over all.
Serves 6

MINCEMEAT

approximately 2-1/2 pounds calves'
  or pigs' feet
4 pounds finely chopped apples
1-1/2 pounds currants, washed and
  drained
1-1/2 pounds raisins
2 pounds brown sugar
1 pound suet, finely chopped
1 quart apple cider
1 pint brandy
1 teaspoon whole cloves
1 whole nutmeg, freshly grated
1 cup orange juice
3 tablespoons grated orange rind
1/3 cup lemon juice
1 tablespoon grated lemon rind
1/2 cup candied orange peel
1/2 cup candied lemon peel
1 cup candied citron
1/2 teaspoon freshly ground pepper
1 teaspoon salt

Prepare feet according to Steps I and II in basic instructions cooking in salted water until tender, about 1-1/2 hours. When cool enough to handle, remove bones and press meat through a colander. When cold, press through colander once again.

Meat should resemble pearl barley. Mix meat thoroughly with all other ingredients (except salt and pepper). Store in refrigerator for 3 days to blend flavors before using. Then divide into pints or quarts and freeze. Use as needed. Add salt and pepper to each 4 cups of mincemeat just before using for pie filling.

Enough for 12 pies; use 2 full cups for each 9-inch pie

109

CHINESE PIGS' TAILS & PEANUT SOUP

1 pound pigs' tails
1 cup raw Virginia peanuts or
    blanched almonds
1 slice fresh ginger root
1 tablespoon choong toy* (salted,
    preserved turnip)
1 teaspoon salt
1/2 cup chopped green onions,
    with tops

Clean and parboil pigs' tails according to Steps I and II in basic instructions; cut in 2-inch lengths. Return to the pot with 2 quarts fresh water and all the remaining ingredients except green onions. Bring to a boil, reduce heat, cover and simmer for 1-1/2 hours. Add the green onions just before serving.
Serves 6 to 8
*Available in Oriental markets

BARBECUED PIGS' TAILS

We attribute this recipe to the Mennonite colony of Ontario. It's often served at picnics and is known as one of the favorite foods at stag parties.

2 dozen pigs' tails
2 tablespoons olive oil
1 cup tomato sauce
1/4 cup tomato paste
1/4 cup brown sugar or syrup
2 tablespoons wine vinegar
1 teaspoon Worcestershire sauce
juice of 1 lemon
1 clove garlic, finely chopped
1 teaspoon dry mustard
salt and freshly ground pepper to taste
1/2 teaspoon rosemary (optional)

Prepare pigs' tails according to Step I in basic instructions; cut in 3-inch pieces. Place pigs' tails on a rack and bake in a 300° oven for 2 to 3 hours, until meat is tender and most of fat has baked off. An alternate method to this is to simmer the pigs' tails in acidulated water for 1-1/2 hours. Combine all other ingredients for barbecue sauce, coating tails well. Grill over hot charcoal, turning and basting, until crisp. If fresh rosemary is available, break off several branches, tie them together and use as a basting brush. For barbecuing, we prefer leaving the tails uncut or halved, so as to have fewer pieces to constantly turn.
Serve with traditional barbecue accompaniments such as corn-on-the-cob, French bread and green salad.
Serves 6 to 8

PIGS' TAILS & LIMA BEANS

12 pigs' tails, cut in 2-inch pieces
1 pound dried lima beans, washed
 and soaked overnight
1 onion, sliced
1 clove garlic, finely chopped
2 bell peppers, sliced
1/2 teaspoon dry mustard
1 whole dried red chili
1/4 cup chopped parsley
salt and freshly ground pepper to taste

Prepare pigs' tails according to Step I
in basic instructions. Place in a pot and
cover with water; simmer for 1/2 hour,
skimming to remove any scum. Add all
other ingredients. Cook another 1 to
1-1/2 hours until tender.
Serves 8

Variation: Pigs' ears, snouts and feet
may be substituted for the pigs' tails;
just prepare particular meats according
to basic instructions for cleaning.

LAMBS' TAILS

*The serving of lambs' tails is filled with
wonderful folklore. This particular
recipe roots itself deep into the Basque
culture where sheepherding on the
steppes of the Pyrénées Mountains is a
way of life. In California's San Joaquin
Valley, where there is a large Basque
settlement, picnics traditionally following the "lambing." The bobbing of
the tails and castrating (the Bascos, by
century-old tradition, castrate the
lamb with their mouths) take place at
the same time. The tails are thrown
into huge pots of boiling water,
stripped of their wool and barbecued
on an open fire. Bowls of white beans
in a garlicky vinaigrette, bota bags
filled with wine and rounds of French
bread are always present in unbeliev-
able quantities. Then there is dancing,
even costumes, music, singing.*

100 lambs' tails
3/4 cup olive oil
8 to 10 cloves garlic, finely chopped
1 bunch parsley, finely chopped
1 cup wine vinegar
1/4 cup water
salt and freshly ground pepper to taste

To remove wool from tails, immerse
them in a large pot of boiling water.
Simmer until wool pulls away from
tails easily. Plunge into cold water;
drain. Remove wool by using a clamp
to hold cut end of tail and slipping
wool off over the other end. Wash tails
several times in fresh water; drain.
Place tails in large baking pan with the
oil. Bake, uncovered, in a 325° oven
for 1-1/2 hours, adding the remaining
ingredients during the last 30 minutes.
Turn tails from time to time during
cooking period to keep from sticking
to pan. Tails should be crispy. Serve
with white beans vinaigrette, a tomato,
onion and cucumber salad and French
bread.
Serves 8 to 10

OXTAIL & VEGETABLE SOUP

3 pounds oxtails, disjointed
1 bay leaf
1 onion, chopped
2 leeks, chopped
2 stalks celery with leaves, chopped
3 carrots, scraped and diced
3 turnips, scraped and diced
3 beets, scraped and diced
2 tomatoes, peeled and chopped
2 cups chopped cabbage, spinach
    or Swiss chard
2 sprigs parsley, chopped
2 teaspoons salt
1/2 teaspoon freshly ground pepper

Prepare oxtails according to Step I in basic instructions. Place in a large stock pot with 3 quarts water. Bring to a boil, skimming to remove any scum that forms. Add the remaining ingredients; cover and simmer for 1-1/2 hours or more. Adjust seasonings and remove bay leaf. Serve in large soup bowls with the oxtails.
Serves 6

Variations: The oxtails may be removed from the stock, drained, dipped in butter, rolled in good French bread crumbs and grilled until crisp.
Pigs' tails may be substituted for the oxtails—just as delicious.

OXTAIL & BLACK BEAN SOUP

2 pounds oxtails, disjointed (about
    2-inch lengths)
1 cup Oriental black beans*, washed
    and soaked overnight
1 slice fresh ginger root
1 piece dried tangerine peel
6 to 8 black forest mushrooms,
    soaked to soften and quartered
    if large
6 to 8 jujube dates** (Chinese
    red dates)
1/4 cup sherry
salt to taste

Prepare oxtails according to Steps I and II in basic instructions. Parboil beans separately for 5 minutes; drain. Combine oxtails and all remaining ingredients, except beans, with 3 quarts of water. Bring to a boil, reduce heat, cover and simmer 1-1/2 hours. Add the beans and continue cooking for another 45 minutes. Adjust seasonings.
Serves 8 to 10
*The black beans called for in this recipe are commonly used by Koreans and other Orientals. They are round, about 1/4 inch in diameter and black throughout, unlike the oval South American black beans with white centers. If unable to obtain Oriental beans, South American black beans may be substituted.
**Available in Oriental markets

OXTAIL & GARBANZO CASSOULET

3 pounds oxtails, disjointed
3 tablespoons olive oil
2 cloves garlic, finely chopped
1 onion, chopped
2 cups beef stock
1 cup chopped fresh fennel,
    including tops
1/2 teaspoon crushed oregano
salt and freshly ground pepper to taste
1 cup diced ham
2 cups cooked garbanzos

Prepare oxtails according to Step I in basic instructions. Heat olive oil in a flameproof casserole, add garlic and onions, and sauté until transparent. Add oxtails, stirring until they have changed color. Add stock, fennel, oregano, salt and pepper. Cover and simmer 1-1/2 hours. Add ham and garbanzos; continue cooking another 30 minutes. Serve hot with French bread and green salad.
Serves 4 to 6

OXTAILS BOURGUIGNON

4 pounds oxtails, disjointed
seasoned flour
1/4 pound bacon, parboiled for
    5 minutes and diced
1 cup beef stock
1 cup dry red wine
bouquet garni (see Basics)
2 tablespoons butter
1 cup fresh pearl onions
1 cup small fresh mushrooms
3 carrots, scraped and cut in
    small chunks
1/2 cup fresh peas
salt and freshly ground pepper to taste
chopped parsley

Prepare oxtails according to Steps I and II in basic instructions; dredge in seasoned flour. Heat bacon in a flameproof casserole, stirring to prevent browning, but allowing fat to be rendered; remove bacon pieces to side. Add the oxtails to the fat and brown well; drain off any excess fat. Return bacon pieces to casserole along with stock, wine and bouquet garni.

Heat butter and sauté onions, mushrooms and carrots quickly. Place in casserole, cover tightly, and cook in a 300° oven for 3 hours. Add peas last 20 minutes of cooking period. Adjust seasonings with salt and pepper. Garnish with chopped parsley.
Serves 4 to 6

Note: This dish may be prepared on top of the stove. Add onions and carrots the last 25 minutes of cooking time, the mushrooms and peas the last 10 minutes. Total cooking time is reduced to 2 hours. If additional liquid is needed, equal parts stock and wine may be added.

SOUR OXTAILS WITH POTATO DUMPLINGS

3 pounds oxtails, disjointed
1 tablespoon vinegar
1 onion, chopped
1 bay leaf
1 teaspoon salt
1/2 teaspoon freshly ground pepper
1 tablespoon flour
1 tablespoon butter
1/4 cup sour cream or yoghurt
potato dumplings (recipe follows)

Prepare oxtails according to Step I in basic instructions. Simmer in 4 cups water along with vinegar, onion, bay leaf, salt and pepper for 1-1/2 hours. Remove bay leaf. Blend together flour and butter, making a beurre manie (see Basics). Stir into soup to thicken, continuing to cook 10 minutes longer. Stir in sour cream at the last minute; serve with potato dumplings.
Serves 4

POTATO DUMPLINGS

1 pound potatoes, boiled until
   tender in their skins
3 tablespoons or more flour
salt
1 egg
1 tablespoon cream

Peel and grate cooled potatoes. Mix with flour on a bread board; make a hollow in the center. Add salt, egg and cream and knead until smooth. Form into a large ball and pinch off small pieces, forming 1-inch balls. Cook in simmering, salted water for 20 minutes; drain. Serve with oxtails.

FILIPINO OXTAIL STEW

5 pounds oxtails, disjointed
3 tablespoons vegetable oil
2 tablespoons annatto (achiote) oil*
1 large onion, thinly sliced
3 cloves garlic, finely chopped
3 quarts beef stock or water
5 tablespoons rice or potato flour,
   toasted
1/2 cup skinned peanuts, finely
   pulverized
1 pound fresh green beans
1 large eggplant, cut in wedges
sliced green onions for garnish

Prepare oxtails according to basic instructions. Heat oil in Dutch oven or flameproof casserole and brown well on all sides. Remove and set aside; discard oil. Add annatto oil to casserole and sauté onion and garlic until transparent, about 6 to 8 minutes. Return oxtails and accumulated juices to casserole. Add stock, bring to a boil, reduce heat, cover and simmer for 2-1/2 hours, until meat is tender. Combine flour and peanuts and gradually stir into casserole. Add green beans and eggplant; turn and coat with liquids. Increase heat and cook, uncovered, for about 15 minutes, stirring occasionally. Garnish with onions. Serve piping hot with rice.
Serves 6

*Annatto (achiote) oil may be purchased in Oriental or Latin American food shops. It's used as a coloring agent and has a taste somewhat like saffron—but infinitely less costly. It is used extensively in Latin America, the West Indies and the Philippines. It may be made by combining seeds (achiote) with twice as much oil and heating a few minutes. Cool and store in a glass jar in the cupboard.

BRAISED OXTAILS, SPANISH STYLE

One of the greatest prizes bestowed upon a toreador after a brave fight in the bullring is the presentation of the bull's ears or tail. It is a culinary prize as well. In Seville, in the heart of grazing bulls and corridas, a restaurant may specialize in a dish called rabo de torro, made from the "sweet" tail meat of the bulls just killed in the ring. It is one of Andalusia's most renowned specialties.

2 oxtails, disjointed (about 3 to 4
    pounds)
3 tablespoons olive oil
2 onions, chopped
2 cloves garlic, finely chopped
1 tablespoon flour
2 cups beef stock
1 cup dry red wine
1/2 cup tomato sauce
6 peppercorns
1/2 teaspoon crushed oregano
1 dried red chili, finely chopped and
    with seeds removed if desired
2 to 3 whole cloves
2 carrots, chopped
1 sweet red pepper, chopped
1 tablespoon chopped parsley
2 potatoes, cut into chunks (optional)
salt and freshly ground pepper to taste

Prepare oxtails according to Steps I and II in basic instructions; drain. Heat oil in large skillet and cook oxtails until browned. Remove from pan and set aside. Add onions and garlic to pan and brown. Add flour and cook 4 minutes; return oxtails to pan. Add stock, wine, tomato sauce, peppercorns, oregano, chili pepper and cloves. Stir to mix, cover and simmer 1-1/2 hours, or until meat is tender. Add carrots, red pepper, parsley and potatoes the last 30 minutes of cooking time.
Serves 6
Note: Meat and potatoes may be removed to a side dish and remaining sauce and vegetables pressed through a sieve. Return sauce to pan with meat and potatoes and heat through.

BRAISED OXTAILS WITH NAPA CABBAGE

2-1/2 to 3 pounds oxtails, disjointed
2 tablespoons corn oil
1 clove garlic, finely chopped
1 slice fresh ginger root,
    finely chopped
2 tablespoons soy sauce
1 teaspoon salt
1/4 teaspoon 5-spice powder
1/4 cup dry sherry
1-1/2 cups beef stock
1 teaspoon cornstarch, mixed with
2 tablespoons water
1 head Napa cabbage or iceberg
    lettuce, cut in wedges

Prepare oxtails according to Steps I and II in basic instructions. Heat oil with garlic and ginger; add oxtails to pan and brown. Add soy, salt, 5-spice powder, sherry and stock. Bring to a boil, reduce heat, cover and simmer 1-1/2 hours, or until meat is tender. Bind juices with cornstarch mixture. Braise cabbage in another pot in salted water for 10 minutes, or until tender; drain. Pour oxtails over wedges.
Serves 6

OTHER OFFAL

Giblets, spleen, lungs, fries, marrow and blood have all been used in a wide variety of cuisines. Yet, except for giblets, they generally have gone unnoticed in the United States.

Fries, marrow and blood are considered delicacies in many countries, especially in Europe. Spleen and lungs, though lacking the prominence and reverence accorded some of the other variety meats, are popular in some cuisines. Giblets, utilized more as a secondary ingredient than the others, are included because they probably are the most commonly used of all the innards.

Most dictionaries define giblets as any visceral organ of fowl. *Larousse Gastronomique* expands this definition to include the head, neck, pinions, feet, liver, cocks' comb and kidneys as well as the heart and gizzard of poultry. (It does exclude the liver of duck and geese, because in France they are given special treatment and are highly valued for their use in pâtés.) Thus it is not so surprising that the French word for giblets, *abatis,* has evolved as the general word for defining all variety meats or innards. We will define giblets to include only the heart and gizzard of any fowl.

Giblets are used for enhancing the flavor of stew or enriching stocks, if they are not cooked in a dish by themselves. One of the most common foods of the Aztecs in Mexico, they were sold by vendors who specialized in prepared poultry giblets of ducks, geese, waterfowl—practically all migratory birds. Along with the flesh and innards of the wild deer, the giblets of fowl were the most common meat in an otherwise mostly vegetarian society.

The spleen, also called melt (miltz by the Jewish populus), and lungs, or lights, most often have been used as ingredients in forcemeats and stuffings, as casings or in soups throughout the course of history. They have never reigned in splendor, but they were never thrown away either. In Renaissance Italy, the spleen, because of its sourness, was thought to be helpful to the stomach and the appetite, though it was thought one may quickly become full when eating it. The bulk of the recipes for spleen and lungs are found in the Slavic, Jewish and Balkan cuisines. Stuffed miltz is a Jewish specialty; lungs are found in the Czechoslovakian beef lungs with sour cream and are used in Hungarian goulash soup.

Lungs used to be readily available at kosher butcher counters in the United States, but in 1971 they were taken off the market. An amendment to the Wholesale Meat Act declared lungs an inedible product, unfit for human consumption. According to the USDA, there is a great deal of bacteria within the lungs that is invisible to the eye, and therefore, undetectable by federal meat inspectors.

Beef and lamb testicles are considered a great delicacy by the French who call them *animelles.* In the United States, beef testicles are commonly called mountain or prairie oysters and lamb testicles are called fries. Fries have been eaten at banquets for centuries in Europe, and have been cooked over open fires by the Basques on the steppes of the Pyrénées. In the United States, the cowboys of the prairies savored both fries and mountain oysters, especially when added to the famous son-of-a-bitch stew. The French, Spanish and Italians seem to be the only people who still recognize fries as a true delicacy. This very delicious meat remains one of the best-guarded culinary secrets of today.

Although rarely prepared by Americans, marrow is often served in European countries. Since the 14th century, it has been a popular first course on a French menu—fried, filled into miniature pastries or made into a pudding—and an important ingredient of sauces such as the *Marchand de Vin.*

It is interesting to note, however, that marrow played an important role in American history. Pemmican, a mixture of dried meat (jerky) pounded with fat, marrow and wild cherries, was the invention of the Cree indians of North America, and became a sustaining food of the explorers. It provided all that was necessary for warmth, energy and nourishment. Today, a lightweight version of pemmican is often carried by backpackers.

Marrow was an important food of the cowboys of the early American West. Commonly called "prairie butter," they piled marrow atop their sourdough biscuits, an excellent substitute for butter. Marrow also belonged to Creole cooking, being part of the "Monday foods"—red beans and rice simmered with a cracked ham marrow bone.

Because the diet of the Eskimos consisted primarily of caribou (a very lean meat), they supplemented it with marrow. They boiled the bones in stews in order to obtain the necessary fat required to maintain body heat in the sub-zero temperatures of Northern Canada.

But the French have brought marrow its greatest fame. In one form or another—fried, baked, rubbed into or laid on top of tender meat, or stirred into sauces—marrow is served in practically every household in France today.

Blood played an important role in ancient rituals. In *Critias,* one of Plato's *Dialogues,* a description of the ancient island of Atlantis is given. Every four or five years the 10 kings who ruled the island met to discuss common affairs and the transgression of laws. They then slew one of the bulls that freely roamed in the sanctuary of Poseiden, mixed its blood with wine and drank the wine from golden beakers, vowing never to transgress from the laws again.

Blood was also one of the most characteristic foods of nomadic peoples. The Berber tribes of the ninth century drained blood from the veins of their cattle, mixed it with milk and drank it, while the Mongolian armies, carrying few provisions and traveling where food was scarce, tapped the veins of their steeds every 10 days or so and drank the blood uncooked. The Arabs, however, cooked the blood from their camels over an open fire before ingesting it.

Blood puddings were popular at medieval banquets and this popularity has carried over to the present day, especially in England, Ireland and France. Prepared blood (both in puddings and sausages) was one of the first items scrutenized for adulteration when meat inspection began in France in the 1300's. In Ireland in the 17th century, peasants bled their cows and boiled the blood with milk, butter and herbs. Drisheen, a blood pudding now famous in County Cork, is actually a version of this centuries-old dish. The bleeding of horses was also a common practice of early trappers and explorers in the days of the settlement of America. If the blood was not consumed in liquid form, it was preserved with salt, cut into squares and reserved for eating during times of scarcity.

The making of *boudin,* a sausage specialty of the country people of France, is rich in tradition. While the slaughtering of the pigs is done by the men of the family, the preparation of the *boudin* is left to the women. The making of *boudin* coincides with the hog slaughter, which most often is around Christmas, but may continue until Easter. We know of more than one occasion when grilled *boudin* has been enjoyed along with the first green tomatoes from the vine.

A famous Filipino dish is *dinuguan* or "chocolate meat," pork and tripe cooked in blood. Some African tribes still drink fresh blood, or coagulate it and roast it over an open fire.

OTHER OFFAL

HUNTER'S GIBLET SOUP

giblets, wings and necks of
    2 wild ducks
1 onion, quartered
1 slice celery root
1 clove garlic, mashed
1 teaspoon salt
1-1/2 cups cooked rice
1/4 teaspoon freshly grated nutmeg
salt and white pepper to taste
1 teaspoon lemon juice
1 tablespoon butter
1 tablespoon flour

Simmer duck parts with 4 cups water, onion, celery root, garlic and salt for 1 hour, skimming away any scum that rises to the surface. Remove meat from bones and chop along with giblets. Strain stock. Add rice, chopped meat and giblets, seasonings and lemon juice. Blend butter and flour together, add in small bits to the soup and cook several minutes to thicken slightly.
Serves 4

GERMAN GIBLET SOUP

1 pound chicken, goose, turkey or
    duck giblets, including neck and
    feet and wings of small birds
3 tablespoons butter
1 onion, sliced
1 bay leaf
1 carrot, thinly sliced
1 turnip, thinly sliced
1 teaspoon salt
freshly ground pepper
1 cup peeled, seeded and chopped
    tomatoes
3 tablespoons heavy cream

Quarter gizzards and halve livers (if not used for pâté!). Heat butter and sauté meats and onion for 5 minutes. Add 6 cups water, bay leaf, carrot, turnip, salt and pepper; simmer 45 minutes or longer. Remove necks, feet and wings, if used; discard. Add tomatoes and continue simmering for 5 minutes. Carefully stir in cream.
Serves 4

CHICKEN GIBLET SOUP WITH LEMON

3/4 pound chicken giblets
3 stalks celery with tops, sliced
3 cloves garlic, finely chopped
1/3 cup or more lemon juice
1/2 pound zucchini, sliced
1-1/2 cups cooked rice
salt and freshly ground pepper

Clean and rinse giblets well. Place in soup pot with 2 quarts water. Bring to a boil, skimming any scum that rises to surface; add celery, garlic and lemon juice and cover. Simmer for 1 hour. Remove giblets and chop; return to pot. Add zucchini and cook 15 minutes longer. Add the rice just before serving; heat through. Salt and pepper to taste.
Serves 6

Variation: One chicken carcass and its giblets may be substituted for the 3/4 pound giblets. Remove carcass before serving.

CHICKEN GIBLET GUMBO

1 pound chicken giblets, including
   necks
1/2 ham hock
1 bay leaf
1 clove garlic, finely chopped
2 tablespoons butter
1 onion, diced
2 stalks celery including tops, diced
2 bell peppers, diced
2 cups tomatoes, peeled and diced
1 dried red chili, minced (or more)
2 tablespoons chopped parsley
1/4 pound okra, sliced

Place giblets and necks in pot with ham hock, bay leaf, garlic and water to cover. Bring to a boil, reduce heat, cover and simmer for about 30 minutes. Remove giblets and chop coarsely; return to pot. Heat butter in skillet and sauté onion, celery and peppers for 5 to 8 minutes. Then add to pot along with remaining ingredients; cook until okra is tender and stew is thickened. Remove necks, ham hock and bay leaf. Serve with rice and a green salad.
Serves 6

WON TONS

1/2 pound lean ground pork
1/4 pound raw shrimp, shelled
   and minced
1/2 teaspoon fried sesame oil*
1 teaspoon soy sauce
1 teaspoon dry sherry
1 tablespoon cornstarch
2 tablespoons minced green onions
1 egg
won ton skins* as needed,
   about 1 pound

Blend together all ingredients (mixture should be moist) and use for filling won ton skins. To fold won tons for soup: Place 1/2 teaspoon filling on lower right corner of won ton skin and roll to center, forming a triangle. Pinch close to filling, holding it in. Now pull the two acute angles down toward each other, keeping triangle flat. Pinch together at center, sealing with a drop of water. The ends remain free, resembling the tails or fins of a fish.
Bring 3 quarts water to a boil and drop in the won tons. When they rise to the top, boil another minute or 2. Drain, rinse with cool water and add to soup as directed in recipe.
*Available in Oriental markets

WAH WON TON

2 quarts clarified chicken stock
1 slice fresh ginger root
8 black forest mushrooms, soaked to
   soften and sliced
6 chicken gizzards, sliced lengthwise
   1/8 inch thick
6 chicken hearts
6 chicken livers, halved
1/2 cup sliced bamboo shoots
1/2 cup sliced water chestnuts
1/4 pound sugar peas (Chinese
   pea pods)
salt to taste
won tons (preceding)

Prepare won tons according to preceding recipe. Combine stock, mushrooms, ginger, gizzards and hearts in a pot; simmer for 30 minutes. Add livers, bamboo shoots and water chestnuts and simmer another 10 minutes. During last 5 minutes of cooking period, add sugar peas and won tons; add salt to taste.
Serves 6
Note: Any combination of squid, abalone, shrimp, chicken or roast pork may be added to stock.

OTHER OFFAL

RAGOUT OF CHICKEN GIBLETS

1 pound chicken giblets, halved
2 tablespoons vegetable oil or
    rendered chicken fat
1 onion, chopped
2 tablespoons chopped parsley
1 teaspoon cumin
2 cups chicken stock
2 potatoes, peeled and diced
1/4 cup lemon juice
1 egg, beaten
2 tablespoons chopped fresh dill

Heat oil and sauté onion until transparent; add giblets and sauté until lightly browned. Add parsley, cumin and stock; cover and simmer for 30 minutes. Add potatoes and cook until tender. Stir in lemon juice. Pour 1/2 cup of cooking liquid slowly into egg, stirring constantly. Gradually add egg mixture to giblets. Stir in dill at last minute.
Serves 3 to 4

SAUTÉED GIZZARDS & HEARTS

1-1/2 pounds chicken gizzards
    and hearts
2 tablespoons flour
4 tablespoons butter or rendered
    chicken fat
1 teaspoon salt
1/4 teaspoon thyme
freshly ground pepper
1/4 cup dry sherry or white wine
1/4 cup chicken stock
1 clove garlic, finely chopped
1 bell pepper, chopped
3 tablespoons chopped parsley
    for garnish

Clean giblets by trimming away any excess fat, dust with flour and brown in melted butter. Add remaining ingredients except bell pepper and parsley. Cover and simmer 1 hour. Add bell pepper during last 15 minutes of cooking time. Garnish with parsley and serve with rice or bulghur wheat.
Serves 4

Variation: For a Hungarian sauté, follow the above recipe, adding 1 teaspoon Hungarian paprika during cooking period. Then sauté 1/2 pound mushrooms in 2 tablespoons butter and add along with bell peppers. Stir in 1/2 pint sour cream just before serving and heat through; do not boil. Serve on buttered noodles.

CHICKEN GIBLET RISOTTO

2 cups diced chicken giblets
4 tablespoons butter or rendered
    chicken fat
1/2 cup chopped green onions
1 cup uncooked rice
3 cups hot chicken stock
pinch of saffron
1-1/2 teaspoons grated orange rind
salt and freshly ground pepper
1/2 cup diced sweet red or bell pepper

Heat butter and sauté giblets, onions and rice for 10 to 15 minutes. Place in a 1-1/2-quart casserole. Dissolve saffron in hot stock and pour into casserole along with orange rind and seasonings. Cover and place in a preheated 350° oven for 45 minutes. During last 15 minutes of cooking period, add sweet peppers. Fluff with fork before serving.
Serves 4

STEAMED CHICKEN HEARTS & GIZZARDS

1 pound chicken hearts and gizzards
1 tablespoon soy sauce
1 tablespoon dry sherry
1 tablespoon peanut oil
1/2 teaspoon finely minced fresh
 ginger root
1/2 cup diced ham
1 tablespoon finely minced choong
 toy* (preserved turnip)
1/2 cup dried lily flowers*, soaked
 10 minutes to soften and tied
 in knots
1 tablespoon cornstarch

Slice gizzards lengthwise 1/8 inch thick. (If desired, hearts or gizzards may be used individually rather than combined.) Combine all ingredients in a shallow, ovenproof dish; spread mixture evenly over bottom of dish, making a slight indention in the center. Place dish in a large steamer filled with water at least 2 inches deep. Cover with tight-fitting lid and steam for 45 minutes. (If steamer not available, remove ends from a tuna can, place in large pot and set ovenproof dish on top of the can.)

Serve with hot rice and a simple vegetable stir-fry, such as bok choy or Napa cabbage.

Serves 4

*Choong toy and dried lily flowers may be purchased at Oriental markets. Lily flowers are also known as golden needles and banana flowers.

BRAISED CHICKEN GIZZARDS

1 pound chicken gizzards, with fat
 (at least 3 tablespoons)
2 tablespoons soy sauce
2 tablespoons dry sherry
1 tablespoon sugar
1 slice fresh ginger root, finely minced
1 piece dried tangerine peel, soaked
 to soften and finely minced
1 cup chicken stock
2 whole star anise
1 teaspoon salt
1 tablespoon cornstarch, mixed with
2 tablespoons cold water

Remove excessive fat from gizzards and reserve. Cut gizzards into 2 lobes (at center connective tissue). Then make crosswise slashes, 1/8 inch deep, on rounded side of each lobe.

Combine soy, sherry, sugar, ginger and tangerine peel and marinate gizzards for 1 hour. Render fat and heat to sizzling; add marinated gizzards, stir-frying until lightly browned, about 5 to 8 minutes. Add stock, star anise and salt. Bring to a boil, reduce heat, cover and simmer for 30 minutes. Thicken juices with cornstarch mixture. Serve with hot rice or on toothpicks for an hors d'oeuvre.

Serves 4 as an entrée

For a chicken gizzard stew: Follow the above recipe, adding sliced carrots, turnips, potatoes and celery to the gizzards after 20 minutes of cooking. Continue to cook until vegetables and gizzards are tender. Bind juices only if necessary.

For braised chicken gizzards with black bean sauce: Follow the above recipe, adding 1 tablespoon fermented black beans, mashed, to the marinade. Omit star anise.

GEFILTE MILTZ
(Stuffed Spleen)

1 beef spleen
2 tablespoons rendered chicken fat
1 onion, chopped
1/2 cup chopped bell pepper
1/2 cup chopped celeriac or celery
2 eggs
2 matzos, soaked in water for
    5 minutes and drained
2 tablespoons chopped parsley
1 teaspoon salt
1/2 teaspoon freshly ground pepper
1 pig's caul* (omit for Kosher
    preparation)
2 cups beef stock

*Pig's caul is the fatty membrane invest-
ing the intestines.

Remove outer membrane from spleen and make a lengthwise pocket. Scrape away 1/2 cup meat from inside of pocket; reserve. Heat fat and sauté onion, bell pepper and celeriac for 2 minutes. Combine eggs with matzos and scraped meat from spleen in a mixing bowl. Add the sautéed vegetables, parsley and season, mixing well. (Mixture will resemble a thick batter.) Stuff this mixture into pocket; skewer or truss with white string. Cover with a piece of caul fat. Place on rack of shallow roasting pan and pour stock over top. Bake in a 350° oven for 1-1/2 hours, basting occasionally. Remove spleen and reduce cooking liquid, or thicken with cornstarch dissolved in cold water. Serve sauce with baked spleen sliced in 1-inch-thick slices.
(For kosher preparation, rub prepared spleen with a tablespoon or more chicken fat or margarine before baking, rather than wrapping in caul fat.)
Serves 4 to 6

Variation on Stuffing

2 tablespoons butter
1 onion, chopped
2 stalks celery, chopped
1 cup sliced cooking apples
1/2 cup soft bread crumbs or diced
    raw potatoes
1/3 cup raisins, soaked in apple
    cider to soften
1 egg
1 teaspoon salt
1/2 teaspoon freshly ground pepper
2 cups apple cider for cooking liquid

Follow the preceding recipe for preparation of spleen. Sauté vegetables and combine with remaining substituted ingredients. Wrap in caul fat and pour apple cider over spleen. Continue as in preceding recipe.

PREPARATION OF FRIES

The culinary term for the testicles of male animals is fries or mountain or prairie oysters in the United States, or *animelles* in France. Generally speaking, the testicles of beef are called mountain or prairie oysters and the testicles of lamb are called fries, though the term fries is sometimes used to refer to both beef and lamb. They are available, if ordered in advance, from some butchers.

Step I: Cleaning and Rinsing
To clean fries, remove the outer skin or sac by slicing through sac near the testicle (or head). Push testicle through slit in sac. Separate sac from testicles by cutting the connecting duct away from testicle. Discard sac. Rinse in cold running water until water runs clear. Drain well.

Step II: Parboiling
Parboil in salted water (1 tablespoon salt for each quart of water) 5 minutes for lamb, 15 minutes for beef. Drain well before using.

SAUTÉED FRIES

Fries from small animals, such as veal or lamb, should be cleaned first, then rolled in flour and dipped into beaten egg. Roll another time in fine French bread crumbs and then sauté in butter until brown.

Fries from large animals, such as beef, should be cleaned and split in half lengthwise. Then marinate fries in an herb-flavored vinaigrette for an hour or so. Roll in a mixture of flour and cornmeal and fry in hot deep fat until golden brown. Salt and pepper to taste. Serve with lemon wedges.

BRAISED MOUNTAIN OYSTERS AND BROCCOLI

1/2 pound mountain oysters
1 clove garlic, minced
1 slice fresh ginger root, minced
1 tablespoon soy sauce
2 tablespoons dry sherry
1 tablespoon sugar
2 slices bacon, diced
1 onion, sliced
1-1/2 pounds broccoli, broken into flowerets and stems trimmed and sliced 1/4 inch thick
1 tablespoon cornstarch, dissolved in 1/4 cup water

Prepare mountain oysters according to Steps I and II in basic instructions. Slice in half lengthwise, then in 1/8-inch slices. Marinate the slices with the garlic, ginger, soy, sherry, and sugar for 30 minutes. Stir-fry the bacon in its own fat, add onions and marinated meat until meat is well seared and brown. Add 3/4 cup water, cover and cook over medium heat for 15 minutes; then add broccoli and cover again until steam rises to top, keeping broccoli tender-crisp. Thicken juices with the cornstarch mixture. Serve with hot rice.
Serves 4

LAMB FRIES CLEROU

1 quart lamb fries
2 tablespoons butter
3 strips bacon, diced
1 onion, chopped
3 or more cloves garlic, finely chopped
1/2 cup chopped parsley
1/2 cup tomato sauce
1/2 cup dry white wine
1/2 cup beef stock
1/2 teaspoon summer savory or rosemary
salt and freshly ground pepper to taste
1 or more dried red chilis, finely chopped
2 tablespoons Madeira or Cognac

Prepare lamb fries according to Steps I and II in basic instructions. Melt butter and render bacon in large skillet. Sauté onion, garlic and parsley for 5 minutes. Add fries and brown. Combine tomato sauce, wine and stock and pour in just enough liquid to barely cover the fries. Add seasonings. Simmer over low heat for 45 minutes, adding more liquid as necessary. At end of cooking period deglaze skillet with Madeira or Cognac. Serve with crusty French bread and a green salad. Serves 6

PREPARATION OF MARROW

Marrow is savored for its rich and creamy flavor and is served closer to its natural form than any other offal. The best marrow comes from leg bones and is often used as a flavor enrichment for soups, stews and sauces. But nothing could be better than spreading marrow on French bread and toasting it under the broiler. When the marrow has melted (the fat content is high), remove and sprinkle with freshly cracked pepper, salt and lemon juice. Serve piping hot.

If you prefer, the marrow bones (about 1-1/2 to 2 inches long) may be baked in the oven at 350° for 25 to 30 minutes (or broiled for a shorter time), and served along with toast or sourdough French bread. Each person then removes marrow from bones.

SUGGESTIONS FOR SERVING MARROW

• Rub marrow into lean meats for added flavor and to keep them from drying out. For instance, sliced liver steaks, heart or kidneys may be rubbed with marrow, cracked pepper and garlic before broiling.

• Serve baked marrow bones for a first course along with toast points.

• When broiling a steak, place a slice of marrow on it after it is turned.

MARROW DUMPLINGS

4 tablespoons fresh marrow (scraped from bone cavity of leg or shank bones preferably)
2 tablespoons butter
2 eggs, beaten
1/2 teaspoon salt
dash of freshly ground pepper
1/4 teaspoon freshly grated nutmeg
2 tablespoons minced parsley
approximately 1 cup fine bread or cracker crumbs
1/2 teaspoon baking powder
stock as needed

Combine all ingredients, except stock, and beat until smooth, adding enough bread crumbs for mixture to hold its shape. Shape into 1/2-inch balls. Cook in boiling stock for 10 to 15 minutes. Remove with slotted spoon. Serve with plain stock or with stewed chicken and vegetables.
Serves 4

MARROW & APPLE PIE

1/2 cup raisins
1/2 cup Calvados, rum or Port
5 pounds marrow bones
1 teaspoon salt
2 pounds tart baking apples
1/2 cup sugar
1 tablespoon cornstarch
pastry for 10-inch pie (page 136)

APPLE PARER.

Soak raisins in Calvados. Put marrow bones on a baking sheet and place in a 350° oven for 15 minutes. Scoop marrow from bones when cool enough to handle, slice and sprinkle with salt.

Peel and slice apples. Line pie dish with pastry. Add apples, sugar, cornstarch, marrow and raisins with Calvados; cover with top crust. Bake for 15 minutes in a preheated 425° oven; reduce heat to 350° and cook for about 45 minutes, or until crust is golden and apples are tender.

SANGUETTE

This is a popular dish in the country where people kill their own chickens and rabbits. In France, you'll even find sanguette available in provincial restaurants. It's a specialty of Orne, in the province of Normandy.

A chicken or rabbit is bled into a dish containing garlic and parsley, even a strip of bacon on occasion. Then the fresh blood is quickly fried in goose fat or lard. Remove to a heated shallow platter and deglaze pan with 1 tablespoon or more cider vinegar. Pour over fried blood and serve with French bread or toast rounds.

DRISHEEN

This is a traditional black or blood pudding from County Cork. Since Ireland was once a country of grazing sheep, it only follows that the first drisheen was made from fresh sheep's blood. Pig's blood may be substituted.

1 quart fresh sheep's or pig's blood
2 cups cream or rich milk, scalded
  and cooled
1/2 cup oatmeal
1/2 teaspoon freshly ground pepper
1 teaspoon salt
1/8 teaspoon mace
1 sprig thyme
pork casings (page 79)

Combine all ingredients and fill into pork casings as per boudin (see page 87). If preferred, mixture may be poured into ramekins or earthenware bowl and baked in a pan of hot water for 1 hour at 300°. Serve warm or cold. This is delicious sliced and fried or grilled for breakfast or supper accompanied by scrambled eggs and rashers (bacon).
Makes about 3 pounds sausages

HUNTERS' BLOOD PUDDING

Any freshly killed bird—a goose, chicken or duck—may fall victim to this recipe.

1 cup fresh blood
1/4 cup rendered poultry fat
3 onions, finely chopped
1/4 cup minced parsley
1 bell pepper, finely chopped
2 cloves garlic, finely chopped
salt and freshly ground pepper

Heat fat and sauté onions, parsley, pepper and garlic. Quickly add blood, sauté, stirring constantly, for 5 minutes. Season to taste with salt and pepper. Serve hot on buttered pumpernickel or black bread with mustard and pickles for a first course; add grilled tomatoes, cheese and fruit for a light supper.
Serves 4 to 6

MIXED MEAT FONDUE

This is a different version of the familiar beef fondue. Select several innards—cubes of calf liver, whole chicken livers, quartered lamb or cubes of veal kidneys, parboiled slices of sweetbreads and brains—and arrange on a platter; garnish with watercress. Combine equal amounts sweet butter and cooking oil in a fondue pot and heat to sizzling. Place the fondue pot over an alcohol burner on the table along with the platter of meats and fresh vegetables such as whole mushrooms and chunks of bell pepper. Each guest makes his own selections and sizzles them to his liking. Have a selection of sauces and/or condiments for dipping—Béarnaise sauce, horseradish blended into whipped cream, Dijon-style mustard, dill-flavored sour cream, chutney, sea salt and freshly cracked pepper. Then, of course, lots of crusty French bread and red wine.

EASTER LAMB
(Stuffed Suckling Lamb)

The traditional Easter meat in Greece is a spit-roasted suckling lamb, filled with a rice stuffing to which almost all the innards—heart, liver, sweetbreads, etc.—are added. The Greeks aren't newcomers to the barbecue. It dates back over 3000 years to the days of Homer.

1 8- to 10-pound suckling lamb,
    cleaned, with head, neck and
    feet removed
salt
juice of 1/2 lemon
4 tablespoons butter
1 lamb heart, chopped
2 lamb kidneys, chopped
1 onion, chopped
1/2 cup rice
2 tablespoons chopped fresh mint
2 tablespoons chopped parsley
1/8 teaspoon cinnamon
1/4 teaspoon freshly ground pepper
1 cup chicken stock
1/2 cup raisins, plumped in dry
    white wine
1 cup tomato juice
branches of fresh oregano or rosemary

Wash lamb inside and out; pat dry. Rub inside cavity with salt; then rub salt and lemon juice into outside flesh. Heat butter in large saucepan and sauté heart and kidneys until lightly browned. Add onion and cook until transparent. Then add rice, herbs, spices and stock. Simmer, uncovered, until most of liquid is absorbed. Then cover and cook for 20 minutes. Stir in raisins. Stuff this mixture into cavity of lamb and truss with white string or skewer together securely.

Cook on a turning spit. Tie branches of oregano together and use for basting brush; baste with tomato juice once meat starts to brown. Grill over glowing charcoal for 1-1/2 to 2 hours. Or, place in a roasting pan in a 300° oven, allowing about 40 minutes per pound. Baste with tomato juice once meat starts to brown. Serve with a Greek salad, bread and wine. A sumptuous feast.

Serves 6 to 8

MIXED LAMB KEBAB

1 pound lamb liver
1 pound lamb heart
1 pound lamb kidneys (prepare
    according to Steps I and II,
    Kidneys)
1/2 cup finely minced onions
2 cloves garlic, finely chopped
1/2 cup lemon juice
1/4 cup olive oil
1/2 teaspoon cracked pepper
4 slices bacon, cut in 1-inch pieces
1 small eggplant, unpeeled and
    cut in 1-inch chunks
1/2 pound zucchini, cut in
    1-inch chunks
flour
light batter (see fritto misto,
    page 132)
oil for deep-frying

Remove arteries and veins from hearts. Cut all meats in 1-inch chunks. Combine onions, garlic, lemon juice, olive oil and cracked pepper and marinate meats for 2 hours. Drain, then skewer alternately with bacon, eggplant and zucchini.

Dust lightly with flour and dip in the prepared batter. Fry in hot, deep fat until crisp and golden. Serve with fresh tomatoes, dressed in a sweet basil or coriander vinaigrette.

Serves 8 to 10

Variation: To barbecue kebabs follow the above recipe, omitting batter. Blanch zucchini for 1 minute or cut in 1/2-inch chunks before threading on skewers. Grill over hot charcoal, basting frequently with remaining marinade, for 5 to 7 minutes on each side.

MIXED MEAT KEBABS

Heart, kidneys and liver—of any variety and in any combination—make particularly good kebabs. Cut meats into 1- to 1-1/2-inch cubes (leave chicken innards whole) and thread on metal or bamboo skewers. Marinate for at least 3 hours to adequately tenderize and flavor meat. Grill over hot charcoal, basting often and turning and being especially careful not to overcook.

You may also alternate the meats with mushroom slices, bell pepper chunks, cherry tomatoes, bacon strips (for extra moisture), Bermuda onion chunks, pearl onions (parboiled 5 minutes), sweet pepper chunks or whatever else sounds good.

Each of the following marinades is sufficient for 3 pounds of meat. Combine all ingredients listed and marinate meats for at least 3 hours, or overnight in the refrigerator.

HERB MARINADE

1 cup olive oil
1/2 cup red wine
2 onions, chopped
2 sprigs thyme
2 bay leaves
1 teaspoon freshly ground pepper
1/2 teaspoon salt
3 cloves garlic, finely chopped

TURKISH MARINADE

1/2 cup olive oil
1/2 cup lemon juice
1/2 teaspoon cinnamon
salt and freshly cracked pepper

CHINESE MARINADE

1/4 cup soy sauce
1/4 cup sherry
2 tablespoons corn oil
1/2 teaspoon fried sesame oil*
2 cloves garlic, finely chopped
1 teaspoon finely chopped fresh
  ginger root
1 teaspoon sugar
1 tablespoon chopped fresh
  coriander (optional)
1 tablespoon chopped green onions

Variation: Omit soy sauce; add 1/4 cup hoisin sauce and 1/2 teaspoon 5-spice powder.
*The dark seasoning oil available in Oriental markets.

GREEK MARINADE

1/2 cup olive oil
1/3 cup lemon juice
2 onions, finely minced
2 bay leaves, crushed
1 teaspoon crushed oregano
3/4 cup sieved tomato pulp
salt and freshly cracked pepper

YOGHURT MARINADE

1/2 pint plain yoghurt
1/2 cup chopped fresh mint
1 onion, finely minced
2 cloves garlic, minced
salt and freshly cracked pepper

ENGLISH MIXED GRILL

6 rib lamb chops
6 small slices calf liver, brushed
    with butter
12 large mushroom caps, brushed
    with butter
6 slices bacon
6 lamb kidneys, split
6 tomatoes, halved
fried shoestring potatoes
watercress for garnish

Broil lamb chops, liver and mushrooms 4 to 5 minutes on each side. Broil bacon until crisp. Then broil kidneys and tomatoes a total of 5 minutes. Place fried potatoes in the center of a large platter; surround with meats and tomatoes. Garnish with watercress. Serves 6

FRITTO MISTO

This famous Italian mixed fry is made up of an assortment of variety meats— chicken and calf liver, kidneys, brains, sweetbreads—and may include chunks of chicken breast or veal as well. Like the Japanese tempura, vegetables are very much a part of the dish. Artichoke hearts, slices of zucchini and eggplant, mushrooms and/or cauliflowerets are served along with the meats. Cut all the selected foods in equal-sized pieces. The sweetbreads, brains and vegetables should be parboiled. All of the ingredients are then dipped into a rich batter and fried in deep, hot fat (380° on a frying thermometer) until golden. Generally speaking, the fat is a combination of olive oil and sweet butter (about 1-1/2 quarts olive oil to 1/2 cup butter). It is essential to maintain a hot temperature; reduced temperatures and crowding cause sogginess. As foods are fried, remove to a warm platter and serve immediately. When all the ingredients have been fried, sprinkle with salt and serve with lemon wedges.

BATTER

1 tablespoon melted butter
2 eggs, well beaten
2/3 cup milk or cream
1 cup flour
1/2 teaspoon salt
1/4 teaspoon white pepper

Combine all ingredients and beat until smooth. Let batter stand about 20 minutes before using. Dry all meats well before dipping them into batter.

SON-OF-A-BITCH STEW

Although there is great controversy concerning the ingredients that go into the S.O.B. stew, there is one ingredient that all cooks regard indispensable. That is the marrow gut called "marguts," by the old range cooks. According to an old saying: "A son-of-a-bitch may have no brains and no heart and still be a son-of-a-bitch. But if it don't have no guts, it's not a son-of-a-bitch." The Texas cooks of the chuck wagon claim this stew as their contribution to the culinary hall of fame. Cowboys, range cooks and Texans alike wax poetic over its unforgettable flavor. And the stories are endless, as you can well imagine.

2 pounds beef chuck, flank or brisket
1 oxtail, disjointed
1 pound tripe
1 beef heart
1 tongue
1/2 pound mountain oysters (optional)
1 pound sweetbreads
1 pound veal or lamb kidneys
1/2 pound liver (optional)
1 pound calf brains
1-1/2 pounds marrow gut
(intestine of an unweaned calf)
1/3 pound beef kidney suet
3 or more dried red chilis, chopped
1 teaspoon oregano leaves
1 teaspoon sage leaves
2 tablespoons salt
1/2 teaspoon freshly ground pepper

Clean and dice all meats in 1/2-inch cubes, with the exception of the oxtail and brains. Prepare brains according to Steps I and II in basic instructions; leave whole. Place chuck, oxtail, tripe, heart, tongue, mountain oysters, marrow gut and suet in a large pot with chilis, oregano, sage, salt and pepper. Pour in water just to cover (or part coffee and part water). Bring to a boil, skimming away any scum that rises to the surface. Cover and simmer 3 hours. Remove tongue, skin and dice in 1/2-inch cubes. Return to pot with sweetbreads, kidneys, liver and brains. Stir into other meats, cover, and simmer for another 20 minutes. Serve hot in deep bowls with sourdough biscuits or bread and a green salad.
Serves 12 generously

BASICS

BEURRE MANIE

To make a beurre manie, use your fingers to combine the flour and butter, making a crumbly mixture. Sprinkle the grains gradually into hot liquid. Use for thickening soups and sauces.

BOUQUET GARNI

2 to 4 sprigs parsley
1/4 teaspoon thyme
1 small bay leaf

Wrap herbs together in a piece of washed cheesecloth and tie securely. Use for flavoring stocks, soups, stews, sauces and braised meats.
Note: Additional herbs may be added to the bouquet garni, if desired, including chervil, tarragon, rosemary, basil, etc.

CORNING OR PICKLING BRINE

To each gallon of cold water add:
1-1/2 cups rock salt or sea salt
1 cup dark brown sugar
2 to 3 tablespoons saltpeter*
any combination of spices such as
    whole peppercorns, allspice, cloves,
    bay leaves, garlic cloves, fresh
    ginger slices, crushed juniper
    berries, mustard seeds and
    blades of mace

Boil all ingredients for 5 minutes. Allow to cool and strain before pouring over meat.
Note: One of our favorite combinations of spices is 2 bay leaves, 8 peppercorns and 4 crushed juniper berries. *Saltpeter is available at most drugstores, labeled as sodium nitrate. It is responsible for the pink color taken on by the meat.

VINAIGRETTE DRESSING

3/4 cup olive oil
1/3 cup wine vinegar
1 tablespoon lemon juice
1 teaspoon salt
freshly ground pepper to taste
1 teaspoon finely chopped chives
1 tablespoon finely chopped parsley
1/2 teaspoon tarragon

Combine all ingredients and mix well.

Variation: Follow the above recipe, omitting tarragon. Substitute 1 or 2 cloves garlic, finely chopped. Just before serving, stir in 1/4 cup more finely chopped parsley and 2 green onions with tops, finely chopped. This is the same vinaigrette the Basques use for their white beans. The additional parsley and green onions are stirred into the already marinated beans just before serving.

BASICS

BÉCHAMEL SAUCE

2 tablespoons butter
4 tablespoons minced onion
4 tablespoons flour
1 cup court bouillon or stock
1 cup milk

Melt the butter in a pan, add onions and cook for 2 minutes. Then add flour, blend well and cook another 2 minutes. Gradually add the stock and milk and cook until thickened.
Makes 2 cups

SAUCE GRIBICHE

1 tablespoon Dijon-style mustard or
    to taste
1 tablespoon wine vinegar
3/4 cup olive oil
salt and freshly ground pepper to taste
1 tablespoon chopped fresh herbs
    (parsley, chervil or chives or
    in combination), or
1 teaspoon chopped fresh thyme
1 tablespoon chopped cornichons
2 teaspoons chopped capers
1 hard-cooked egg, yolk finely
    sieved and white cut julienne

Combine all ingredients and mix well. Allow several hours for flavors to blend. Excellent as a garnish for head-cheese, cold cuts, pâtés and terrines.
Makes 1 cup

BÉARNAISE SAUCE

1/2 cup white wine vinegar
1 tablespoon minced shallots or
    whites of green onion
1 tablespoon fresh minced tarragon, or
1 teaspoon dried tarragon leaves
pinch of salt and freshly ground pepper
3 egg yolks
1/4 cup butter

Combine the vinegar, shallots, tarragon, salt and pepper and cook over medium heat until reduced to 2 tablespoons. Do not burn. Cool. In the top of a double boiler, over hot (not boiling) water, beat the egg yolks with the vinegar mixture, using a wire whisk until thick. Add a tablespoon of butter at a time, beating until melted; repeat, until all butter has been added. Serve this sauce lukewarm.
Makes 1-1/2 cups
Note: If this sauce should accidentally curdle (water too hot); let cool to lukewarm and whirl in a blender for a couple seconds.

HOT TOMATO SALSA

1 onion, finely chopped
2 tablespoons olive oil
3 cups peeled, seeded and chopped
    tomatoes
3 tablespoons lemon juice
salt and freshly ground pepper to taste
1 teaspoon grated lemon rind

Sauté onions in olive oil. Add chopped tomatoes and lemon juice; bring to a boil and simmer 5 minutes. Season to taste with salt and pepper. Add the lemon rind and more juice to taste just before serving.
Makes approximately 3-1/2 cups

TOMATO SALSA

2 cups peeled and chopped
    fresh tomatoes
2 long green chilis, peeled
    and chopped
2 tablespoons olive oil
2 tablespoons red wine vinegar
1/2 onion, finely chopped
1 clove garlic, finely chopped
1/2 teaspoon crushed oregano
1 tablespoon chopped fresh coriander
salt and freshly ground pepper to taste

Combine all ingredients, allowing 2 to 3 hours for flavors to blend.
Makes about 1 pint

RICH PIE PASTRY

2 cups sifted unbleached white flour
1 teaspoon salt
3/4 cup Crisco shortening (or part
    butter)
about 4 tablespoons cold water

Combine the flour and salt in a mixing bowl. Cut in the shortening with a pastry blender. Sprinkle the water, a tablespoon at a time, mixing well with a fork until all the flour is moistened. With hands, gather the dough into a ball. Divide in two and roll each ball of dough to 1/8 inch thickness. Fit into pie plate or top pie according to recipe. May be frozen for later use.
Makes 2-crust 9- or 10-inch pie

PUFF PASTRY

2 cups all-purpose flour
1/2 teaspoon salt
1/3 cup ice water
1/2 pound sweet butter, very cold

Sift the flour and salt on a board. Make a well in center. Stir in water with fingers; knead dough until smooth and elastic. Roll dough into a rectangle about 1/4 inch thick. Cut the butter in thirds, lengthwise. Place the butter slices in the center of the dough, the length of the rectangle. Fold one flap over the butter and bring the other flap on top. This makes 3 layers and should cover the butter entirely. Press the side edges together to prevent butter from "oozing" out. Chill the dough for 30 minutes. Place the chilled dough on board and roll into a longer rectangle. Dough should be rolled as thin as possible without the butter coming through. If butter breaks through, it means air is being lost (enclosed air puffs the paste). Fold the rectangle again in thirds, this time "pressed" edges over center, and other edge over top. This is called a "turn." Chill again for 30 minutes. Repeat 4 more times, chilling and rolling after every turn. Dough may be chilled or frozen at this point. Be sure to wrap well with plastic wrap, to prevent drying out in refrigerator or freezer. Use as needed.

VOL-AU-VENT & PATTY SHELLS

Cut out circles on heavy paper to be used as patterns, 2-1/2 inches for patty shells, 6 to 8 inches for vol-au-vent. Roll out puff pastry 1/4 inch thick. Place pattern on top and cut circles with a sharp pointed knife. Place cut dough on paper-covered baking sheet. Cut another circle for each shell the same outside diameter, but cut out center so that only a 1-inch rim remains. Remove center circle and place on baking sheet (for topping baked, filled shell). Moisten surface of pastry circles. Top base circles with rim circles. Brush all surfaces with beaten egg mixed with 1 tablespoon milk. Bake in a preheated 450° oven for 5 minutes. Reduce heat to 375° and bake 25 to 30 minutes. Vol-au-vent shell should be used immediately. Patty shells will keep for 2 days in a dry place; reheat.

REFRIED BEANS
(Frijoles Refritos)

2 cups pinto beans
1/2 teaspoon oregano
salt to taste
8 tablespoons lard
1/4 pound Jack cheese, coarsely
   grated

Wash and soak beans overnight in 2 quarts cold water. Add salt and oregano and simmer in same liquid, covered, until beans are tender, about 1-1/2 hours. (Beans should be well cooked.) Drain, reserving liquid; mash beans well. Place lard in a heavy skillet and bring almost to the smoking point. Carefully add mashed beans and cook over low heat, stirring frequently, until lard is absorbed. More lard may be added if desired. Beans may also be thinned out to desired consistency with some ot the reserved cooking liquid. Add cheese, mix well and cook until completely melted. Continue to cook 15 minutes. Use as a side dish or as filling for tortillas, tacos or burritos. Serves 6 to 8
Note: If you prefer spicier beans, sauté onions, garlic and/or dried red chilis in the lard until onions are transparent before adding the beans.

MEXICAN RICE

2 cups rice, washed and well drained
3 to 4 tablespoons lard
1 medium-size onion, chopped
1 or more cloves garlic, minced
1/2 teaspoon cumin
1/4 cup tomato sauce
salt to taste

Sauté rice in melted lard until lightly browned. Add chopped onion, garlic and cumin and continue cooking until onions are limp. Add tomato sauce and salt. Add 3-1/2 cups water to rice. Bring to a rapid boil, lower heat to medium and continue cooking, uncovered, until all the liquid has been absorbed. Then lower heat to simmer, cover and continue cooking for 15 minutes.
Serves 8

SWEET VEGETABLE RELISH

This is a crisp, refreshing relish that is good served with most any meat, but especially barbecued meats such as kebabs.

3 cups carrots, peeled and sliced on
   diagonal 1/8 inch thick
1 large bell pepper, cut in
   1-inch chunks
1 sweet red pepper, cut in 1-inch
   chunks
2 onions, cut in 1-inch chunks
1 cucumber, unpeeled, seeded and
   cut in 1-inch chunks
1/2 cup thinly sliced fresh ginger root
1 or more dried red chilis
1 cup vinegar
1 cup sugar
1/2 teaspoon salt

Prepare all vegetables. Then combine ginger root, dried chilis, vinegar, sugar and salt with 3/4 cup water in a saucepan. Bring to a rapid boil, reduce heat and simmer for 5 minutes; remove from heat, cool to tepid and add carrots. Cool completely, stirring from time to time. Add bell pepper, sweet red pepper, onions and cucumber. Pour into a bowl and chill at least 4 hours, or overnight, in the refrigerator. May be stored in the refrigerator up to 3 days.
Makes approximately 3 pints

INDEX

INDEX

INDEX

ABOUT THE AUTHORS

The collaboration of Jana Allen and Margaret Lee Gin brings together the culinary heritages of Europe and the Far East in the preparation of innards and other variety meats.

Jana Allen, presently assistant food editor of the *San Francisco Chronicle,* was raised in Bakersfield, California, near the large Basque sheepherding community in the foothills of the lower San Joaquin Valley. As a child here she developed an early interest in food and a taste for innards, attending many French-Basque gatherings in which food played a major role. Since graduating from Oregon State University, Jana Allen has traveled extensively in Mexico and Europe, always sampling and studying the cuisines of the countries visited. Before joining the *Chronicle* food staff, she taught a course in Regional and Foreign Foods at San Marin High School in Marin County. Her articles have been published in *Bon Apetit* and other periodicals.

Margaret Gin's culinary background is a unique combination of Chinese and the American West. Her parents were raised in Canton and settled in Tucson, where they owned a grocery store featuring homemade American pastry. As a young girl she mastered the preparation of Chinese stir-fry cooking, while learning to prepare spicy Mexican dishes with equal ease. After moving to San Francisco, her Oriental banquets became so renowned that at friends' urging, she began teaching Chinese cooking classes. This is Mrs. Gin's second book for 101 Productions. The first, *Peasant Cooking of Many Lands,* written in collaboration with Coralie Castle, was published in 1972.